NUMBER TWENTY–ONE

The Career of
Mrs. Anne Brunton Merry
in the American Theatre

LOUISIANA STATE UNIVERSITY STUDIES
MAX GOODRICH, GENERAL EDITOR

HUMANITIES SERIES
PERCY G. ADAMS, EDITOR

Mrs. Merry as Horatia in *The Roman Father*

The Career of
Mrs. Anne Brunton Merry
in the American Theatre

Gresdna Ann Doty

LOUISIANA STATE UNIVERSITY PRESS / BATON ROUGE

ISBN 0–8071–0947–9
Library of Congress Catalog Card Number 74–166970
Copyright © 1971 by Louisiana State University Press
All rights reserved
Manufactured in the United States of America
Printed by Heritage Printers, Inc.
Designed by Albert R. Crochet

To my mother and father

Preface

At the turn of the nineteenth century, Philadelphia was the theatrical center of the United States. It had earned this distinction largely because of its elegant new theatre on Chestnut Street and its excellent resident company of actors. Within a single week performers could provide theatregoers with a favorite classic, a successful holdover from the previous season, and a brand new offering. The success, and indeed the survival, of the company in its early turbulent years can be greatly attributed to Anne Brunton Merry, the artistic pacesetter for actors in the United States between 1796 and 1808. Although she was the most celebrated actress to appear in this country before 1808, she remains a relatively obscure figure. Cultural and theatrical histories contain only cursory and scattered references to her career. In certain respects this is not surprising, because the full story of the development of the American theatre still is being pieced together and, to date, most studies consider only theatre managements and the activities in a given locale. Few studies treat the most dynamic component of eighteenth century theatre, the actor. By tracing the career of an individual performer, Anne Brunton Merry, this study attempts to provide additional insight into the American theatre in its infancy and the conditions under which performers worked.

In following and analyzing Mrs. Merry's career, newspapers from London, Philadelphia, New York, Baltimore, and Washington, as well as long- and short-lived magazines, provided critical accounts and listings of her performances. Published memoirs of fellow actors such as James Fennell, John Bernard, William Wood, and Charles Durang offered firsthand personal and professional observations and evaluations of the actress. A witness to her London debut, professional associate and historian William Dunlap furnished invaluable glimpses into her career. Perhaps the most unusual and significant single source of information was the unpublished journals of Mrs. Merry's third husband William Warren, who kept a daily account of the theatrical operations of the Chestnut Street company beginning in 1796. Continuing the journal the rest of his professional life, Warren provides a daily record of Mrs. Merry's performances as well as box-office receipts and terse personal comments which were especially helpful in reconstructing the professional life of the actress.

Although the study largely concerns Mrs. Merry's twelve-year career as an actress and manager of the Chestnut Street company, the first two chapters discuss her career in the British Isles as a background for understanding her career in the United States. Chapters three through six treat the most significant performances and events of each season in America, and the final chapter attempts to assess her contributions to the development of theatre in the United States and her position in the history of the American stage.

Acknowledgments

I would like to express my gratitude to Professor Percy Adams, the University of Tennessee, for his editorial guidance; to Professor Waldo Braden, Louisiana State University, for his encouragment and help in the final preparation of the manuscript; and to Dean Irwin Berg and the College of Arts and Sciences, Louisiana State University, for the research grant which allowed for revision of the manuscript. A debt is owed as well to Patricia Harris Burgin and to Professor Andrea Goudie, University of Wichita, who read the manuscript carefully in an earlier version and offered valuable critical recommendations.

Above all I am indebted to Professor Hubert C. Heffner, who first suggested the topic, and Professor Oscar G. Brockett, Indiana University, two scholars whose training made the problems of research and analysis immeasurably easier to resolve. I am grateful to them, too, for making the study of the theatre and its history a real pleasure for me.

Contents

Illustrations

The Career of
Mrs. Anne Brunton Merry
in the American Theatre

I
From the Province to the London Stage

The streets adjacent to the theatre were crowded before the opening of the doors, and all the usual consequences of a *rush* ensued. Borne into the pit, we remained wedged in, where the crowd placed us, but we were amply repaid for the sufferings experienced in narrow passes while moved (although motionless from shoulders downward) to the seat we were thrust into. The extraordinary self-possession of this young lady, not yet sixteen, when she appeared at Bristol the preceding year has been recorded by a witness, and it apparently did not desert her on this occasion. Her voice, never exceeded in sweetness and clearness, did not falter, her action was perfect, she was the Horatia of the poet, and London confirmed Mr. Palmer's opinion that she was "another Siddons."[1]

William Dunlap thus records his impression of Anne Brunton who stepped before her first Covent Garden audience as Horatia in *The Roman Father,* October 17, 1785. Dunlap—playwright, manager, and the first American theatre historian—later would observe her in the full maturity of her artistic powers, when she might truly deserve comparison with one of England's great tragic actresses. In the future he would attempt to hire her for his own company, but in 1785 he saw only a talented sixteen-year-old girl who a year before had never stepped before an audience. Her mercurial rise from the Theatre Royal, Bath, to London, did not prepare her to displace or challenge Mrs. Sarah Siddons, reigning queen of the London stage. It did, however, launch Anne Brunton on a successful seven-year engagement at Covent Garden and

---

[1] William Dunlap, *History of the American Theatre* (London, 1833), I, 336–37.

3

prepare her ultimately for a career in the United States, where she became the first great actress to perform on this side of the Atlantic.

Although Anne Brunton spent most of her early years in the provinces, she was born in Drury Lane, Westminster, May 30, 1769. John Brunton, her father, had come to London from his native Norwich to become a grocer and tea-dealer in Drury Lane.[2] Being the son of a soap dealer and having already served a seven–year apprenticeship to a Norwich wholesale grocer, Brunton gave every indication of following a business career. But in April, 1774, a man named Younger, prompter at Covent Garden, encouraged him to appear in a benefit performance for Younger in the title role of Cyrus. Apparently Brunton met with success, for in that same season he also played Hamlet for the benefit of another actor. The two performances seem to have been sufficient encouragement to persuade him to abandon the business world, return to Norwich, and engage himself in the theatre, where he won a reputation as the best actor on that stage.[3] By 1780 Brunton's acting brought him an invitation to join the company at Bath, a move that meant more prestige and greater financial rewards.[4] The new position also had the significant advantage of bringing him in association with the talent of Sarah Siddons, with whom he made his Bath debut as Dumont in *Jane Shore* in the fall of 1780. Brunton played in the same company with the great actress until 1782, when she triumphantly returned to London and a career that would subsequently establish her as one of the finest actresses in the history of the English stage. Brunton remained at Bath for three additional years but eventually returned to Norwich. Never an outstanding actor, he is best remembered as an actor-manager of the Norwich theatre and as founder of a theatrical family which received recognition on both sides of the Atlantic. In addition to his eldest child Anne, two other daugh-

---

[2] *The Thespian Dictionary* (London, 1802), p. ME–MI.
[3] *Ibid.*
[4] Joseph Haslewood, *The Secret History of the Green-Room* (London, 1795), II, 84.

ters and a son became actors. Elizabeth made her first appearance at her sister Anne's benefit in May, 1790, at Covent Garden. Evidently she was not as successful as Louisa, Brunton's sixth daughter, who was born in 1785 and made her debut at Covent Garden in October, 1803. One critic predicted a brilliant future for this beautiful and gifted actress.[5] Instead, she left the stage and married into the nobility, long enjoying the title of Countess of Craven until her death in 1860.[6]

During her entire four-year engagement at Covent Garden, Louisa acted with her brother John, who had made his debut three years before her in September, 1870, as Brunton the Younger. Known as an actor of general use, the younger Brunton also managed theatres at Brighton, Birmingham, Lynne, and Plymouth.[7] His daughter Elizabeth brought the third generation of Bruntons to the stage and married Frederick Yates, an actor-manager at the Adelphi in the early part of the nineteenth century.

The playhouse at Bath provided substantial encouragement to John Brunton and initial theatrical nourishment for his children. Celebrated as the most fashionable spa in Georgian England, the city beckoned royalty as early as 1574, when Queen Elizabeth first visited there. After 1663, the year Charles II brought his royal consort to Bath, the city gradually changed from a town known for its woolen manufacturing to a recognized resort. Visiting royalty, nobility surrounding the court, and commoners wealthy enough to afford the healing natural springs made the Bath audience the most sophisticated in the provinces. The building that would house such glittering audiences and provide the scene for Anne Brunton's debut opened in 1750 through the endeavors of John Palmer (a well-to-do brewer and tallow chandler) and nine other citizens.[8] All that is known of the original plans is that the building was sixty feet long and forty feet wide. In the early years

---

[5] Thomas Gilliland, *The Dramatic Mirror* (London, 1808), II, 689.
[6] *Burke's Genealogical and Heraldic History of the Peerage*, ed. Peter Townend, 103d ed. (London, 1963), 614.
[7] Gilliland, *The Dramatic Mirror*, II, 688.
[8] Belville S. Penley, *The Bath Stage* (London, 1892), 9.

of the playhouse, when it was known as the Orchard Street theatre, the price of admission was 3s for a box, 2s for the pit, 1s6d for
the first gallery, and 1s, upper gallery. Servants were permitted to
go ahead to secure seats for their employers as early as 4 P.M. for
a 6 P.M. performance.

Thirteen years before the Bruntons moved to Bath, Palmer
initiated improvements in the playhouse, possibly to compete
with a new one in nearby Bristol which was modeled after Drury
Lane and could accommodate as many as sixteen hundred spectators.[9] Soon after the renovations Palmer petitioned Parliament
for a patent for his Bath theatre, which thereafter could bear the
title, Theatre Royal, the first provincial theatre so designated.
No doubt its new status increased both prominence and attendance for the theatre, because in 1774 or 1775 the building again
underwent the alterations that gave it the appearance of Anne's
day. The Chestnut Street theatre in Philadelphia, where she
played years later, may have seemed comfortably familiar, for it
was said to have been a perfect copy of the Bath theatre.[10]

Anne Brunton's talent emerged in the flourishing theatrical
environment maintained by Palmer's son, who methodically
toured the principal theatres each year, scouting for new talent
and ideas. Perhaps on one of his tours the younger Palmer noticed
John Brunton at Norwich and engaged him for the 1780 season
at Bath. In much the same manner in 1796, Thomas Wignell,
journeying from Philadelphia to England, engaged Anne for the
Chestnut Street theatre.

Theatrical activity at Bath prospered to such an extent under
the younger Palmer that he leased the neighboring Bristol theatre, for which he also secured a royal patent in 1777. By 1781 he
scheduled performances three times a week in Bristol and once

[9] M. E. Board, *The Story of the Bristol Stage, 1490–1925* (London, 1925), 18.
[10] Charles Durang, "The Philadelphia Stage from the Year 1749 to the Year
1855. Partly Compiled from the Papers of His Father, the Late John Durang
with Notes by the Editors [of the Philadelphia *Sunday Dispatch*]." Philadelphia
Sunday Dispatch, May 7, 1854–July 8, 1860. Chap. II, May 14, 1854. Hereinafter cited as Durang, "The Philadelphia Stage." Durang's attribution has been
challenged by Brooks McNamara, *The American Playhouse in the Eighteenth
Century* (Cambridge, 1969), 105–12.

in Bath, until the fall theatre season began in Bath, when he re-versed the plan.[11] Although the distance between the two cities is short, frequent trips posed transportation problems which Palmer solved by designing two special carriages, one holding fifteen ac-tors, the other twelve.[12] John Bernard, a member of the company for several seasons, recalled that the commuting was "very pleas-ant whilst the fine weather lasted, and created a family-feeling in the company, who, living in both places, would invite each other to beds and breakfast. But when the season advanced, re-turning nine miles at one o'clock in the morning, after a long night's performance, was anything but desirable."[13]

The theatres thrived under Palmer's inventive direction, but there is no evidence that he played a key role in the theatrical art of his company. Both Palmers were businessmen, neither was an actor. They devoted their imaginations and business acumen to management instead and allowed immediate production work to fall to the stage-and acting-manager, the prompter, and box-office keeper.[14] But the Palmer contributions to the Bath theatre were considerable; they helped establish a playhouse, instigated subsequent renovations, secured a royal patent, and united the Bristol theatre with the one at Bath under a single management.

In such a threatrical climate it is not surprising to find talent burgeoning in a provincial actor's offspring. What is unusual is that after the talent of Brunton's daughter was discovered, it was only a brief eight months before the sixteen-year-old girl moved from the provincial stage to Covent Garden, where she remained for seven years. Most London players served apprenticeships in the provinces for several years before arriving on the London boards. Mrs. Siddons, for example, spent no less than four years in Bath before being invited to a permanent position at Drury Lane. Anne's sudden dramatic rise in the theatre resulted from a combination of propitious circumstances: rich natural talent, a

11 John Bernard, *Retrospections of the Stage, 1756–1787* (Boston, 1832), II, 4.
12 *Ibid.*
13 *Ibid.*
14 Penley, *The Bath Stage,* 42.

timely discovery of that talent, and an environment to nourish and develop it.

When John Brunton brought his family to Bath, they settled in a comfortable cottage, where his wife provided the only formal education for their children. Whether he intended theatrical careers for his children is open to dispute. One acquaintance believed that he had no ambitions for them as actors.[15] John Bernard, a family friend as well as a member of the Bath company in which Anne made her debut, claimed her father taught her to read Shakespeare as preparation to become a governess. In contrast, Joseph Haslewood, London writer and antiquarian, asserted that Brunton encouraged and trained his children for the stage, especially Anne.[16] Whether Brunton began early to groom his daughter for the theatre is unknown, but evidence makes clear that she was exposed to Shakespeare as part of her girlhood education at home. She also had the opportunity to see Shakespearean and other plays come alive at the theatre where her father acted. How frequently she attended rehearsals or performances or what actors might have made the strongest impression upon her cannot be determined. One cannot ignore the fact, however, that when Brunton came to Bath, Sarah Siddons was the leading actress and Anne was at the impressionable age of eleven. The young girl must have had many opportunities to observe Mrs. Siddon's techniques and dynamic qualities during the seasons of 1780–1781 and 1781–1782, when she played as many as forty–two different roles in 117 and 129 performances, respectively.[17] She brought to life such Shakespearean characterizations as Desdemona, Portia, Gertrude, and Hamlet. Other roles she frequently performed were Elfrida (*Elfrida*), Cecelia (*Chapter of Accidents*), Almeida (*Fair Circassian*), the Countess (*Count of Narbonne*), Jane Shore and Euphrasia (*The Grecian Daughter*).

[15] Dunlap, *History of the American Theatre*, I, 335.
[16] Bernard, *Retrospections of the Stage*, II, 42; Haslewood, *The Secret History of the Green-Room*, II, 84–85.
[17] John Genest, *Some Account of the English Stage* (Bath, 1832), VI, 211–12, 233–37.

Three years after Mrs. Siddons moved to London, Anne Brunton chose Euphrasia, one of the great actress' most popular characterizations, for her own debut in Bath. It was one of four roles she knew by heart when her father first discovered her talent. Upon returning from rehearsal one day, he heard her reciting one of Calista's speeches. The surprised parent soon discovered that she knew the entire role, as well as those of Juliet, Belvidera, and Euphrasia. Encouraged by John Bernard, her father obtained additional critical evaluation from Palmer, who prophesied that she would be another Siddons.[18] No less than a week later Anne made her debut on the Bristol stage as Euphrasia in Arthur Murphy's sentimental drama *The Grecian Daughter*. Although the play had never won the praise of critics, it had repeatedly moved audiences, awed by the guards' reports of Euphrasia devotedly nourishing her starving father from her own bosom. The role was suited to the actress' age, but it was an extremely challenging part for a novice, demanding the portrayal of tender filial affection, defiance, and anger, climaxed by the slaying of the tyrant Dionysius. Because she chose such a demanding role for her debut, many predicted that Anne would fail.[19] Instead she met with unqualified success, and soon after, on February 17, 1785, she won an equally enthusiastic reception at Bath.[20] On that evening Brunton spoke a special prologue written for the occasion. He assured the audience that if she could not demonstrate sufficient talent that she would withdraw from the stage to become a "plain housewife, not the Tragic Queen."[21] Such a fate may have seemed inevitable when the fledgling actress made her first entrance, for at first the intimidating situation inhibited her powers. But soon, after an early speech drew applause, her energy returned. When she came to the speech in which Euphrasia declares her filial devotion to her father, her sincerity so astonished her listeners

---

[18] Bernard, *Retrospections of the Stage*, II, 43.
[19] Haslewood, *The Secret History of the Green-Room*, II, 85.
[20] Bernard, *Retrospections of the Stage*, II, 43.
[21] "Biographical Sketch of Mrs. Warren," *Mirror of Taste and Dramatic Censor*, I (February, 1810), 121–22.

that they broke into a thunderous response.[22] Bernard remembered that the most surprising feature of her debut was her self-possession; he commented that she moved and spoke with the ease and grace of an experienced player.[23] The next day her performance was acclaimed throughout Bath, and in her subsequent performances that spring she won acclaim for the roles of Euphrasia, Horatia, and Palmira (*Mahomet*) in a dozen appearances. She chose the latter role for her benefit in May, when she received the distinction accorded to Mrs. Siddons of converting part of the pit into boxes.[24] The role of Palmira demands a wide range of emotion, including tender love, scorn, and remorse, as well as a dramatic suicide. For that benefit performance she received £137, handsome testimony to her popularity, especially when compared to some other benefits of the season which amounted to £80 and £72.[25] At another benefit in Bristol on June 13, 1785, she earned an additional £105.

News of her phenomenal success soon reached the ear of Thomas Harris, London's Covent Garden manager, who was seeking new talent. Undoubtedly he hoped to find potential competition for Mrs. Siddons who was attracting large audiences at Drury Lane. He also needed to replace his leading lady Elizabeth Younge, whose marriage to another member of his company, Alexander Pope, made a formidable coalition within the company which any cautious manager would seek to avoid. Consequently Harris did not engage Mrs. Pope the season following her marriage and sought a young and promising actress to portray his tragic heroines.[26] Upon visiting Bath he was sufficiently captivated by what he saw to "entrust the female interest of tragedy to the early excellence of Miss Brunton."[27] In fact, Harris was so eager to hire Anne that he also engaged her father, who under-

---

[22] Haslewood, *The Secret History of the Green-Room*, II, 86–87.

[23] Bernard, *Retrospections of the Stage*, II, 43.

[24] Genest, *Some Account of the English Stage*, VI, 372.

[25] *Ibid.*

[26] James Boaden, *Memoirs of the Life of John Philip Kemble* (London, 1825), I, 290.

[27] *Ibid.*

standably controlled his daughter's early career.[28] Thus, with not
even one complete season of performing experience, Anne accepted a three-year contract with the Theatre Royal, Covent Garden,
for £6 a week.[29] When John Brunton returned to London that
fall, he must have been proud to present his daughter to London
in the theatre of his own debut.

The Theatre Royal, Covent Garden, one of the two patent
theatres of London, was essentially the same structure in 1785 as
when it was first built in 1732 by John Rich, although it had been
remodeled and expanded in 1782.[30] Having the general features of
a Georgian playhouse, it was relatively small, with a fan-shaped
sloping pit containing backless benches and guarded at the sides
of the auditorium by rows of low partitioned boxes. Tiered gal-
leries at the back faced the acting platform, which extended into
the auditorium beyond the side proscenium doors and the first
boxes. In the summer preceding Anne's debut, the theatre was
freshened with paint and gilt, and some of the boxes were removed
to provide more space.[31] Although the Covent Garden season
opened on September 21, Anne did not appear until October 17,
allowing considerable advanced preparation and publicity. The
Daily Universal Register announced that *The Roman Father*,
adapted by William Whitehead from Corneille's *Horace*, would
be revived for Anne's first London appearance. Other daily papers,
eager to find a possible rival for Mrs. Siddons, heaped such indis-
criminate praise on the young actress that it was almost impossible
for her to equal expectations.[32] At the same time, Arthur Murphy
composed a special prologue, the scenic department assembled a
classic setting suggesting Greek architecture, and Mr. Davis, who

[28] "Biographical Sketch of Mrs. Warren," 123.
[29] Charles Beecher Hogan (ed.), *The London Stage* (Carbondale, 1968), V, Pt. 2, 825.
[30] Walley Chamberlain Oulton, *The History of the Theatres of London . . .* (London, 1796), I, 109.
[31] Richard Southern, *The Georgian Playhouse* (London, 1948), 22–32. Special attention is called to a French engraving of G. P. M. Dumont's layout of Covent Garden, 1763, p. 22; Edward Wedlake Brayley, *Historical Accounts of the Theatres of London* (London, 1826), 13; Oulton, *The Theatres of London*, I, 145.
[32] Haslewood, *The Secret History of the Green-Room*, II, 87.

had supplied costumes for Mrs. Pope, designed an elegant dress for Anne. The management also advertised a Roman oration in the fifth act as well as new music composed by William Shield, the Covent Garden musical director.[33]

The tragedy which Anne studied for her extravagantly heralded debut concerns two cities, Alba and Rome, contesting for sovereignty. Horatia, whom Anne portrayed, is torn between her betrothed, representing Alba, and her three brothers, fighting for Rome. In the contest Horatia's lover and two of her brothers are killed. Unable to accept this high price of patriotism, the despairing Horatia, by cursing Rome, provokes her surviving victorious brother Publius into stabbing her. As she dies in the arms of her brother and father, Horatia acknowledges her allegiance to Rome but assures them that death is the only way for her to find peace. James Boaden recalled that at the time he thought it "though an unusual trial part, yet her powers considered, a judicious selection."[34] The characterization was indeed suited to the age of the young actress, but the role would challenge the most accomplished artist, especially in the fifth act when Horatia feigns madness in her frenzied attack against Rome.

By the opening performance the curiosity of the public reached fever pitch, causing "a rush" into the pit. Every part of the house was crowded and an overflow tripled the number of those who got seats.[35] Among the fortunate able to obtain a place was Mrs. Siddons, who must have been curious about her touted rival and pleased by the compliment paid her in the prologue that George Holman delivered to the throng. Despite the elaborate advance publicity, the fledgling did not disappoint her viewers. Her performance brought repeated shouts of approval and applause, especially in the demanding fifth act.[36] Members of the audience agreed that her clear, sweet voice was one of her greatest assets, and Boaden also admired her expressive eyes and her remarkable

[33] London *Daily Universal Register*, October 13, 1785.
[34] Boaden, *Memoirs of John Philip Kemble*, I, 293.
[35] London *Daily Universal Register*, October 18, 1785.
[36] *The Thespian Dictionary*, p. ME–MI.

self-possession.[37] The critic for the *European Magazine* recorded how she must have appeared:

> This young Lady's figure is rather of the under size, but she is nevertheless elegant in her person, and graceful and easy in her action and deportment. Her voice is beautifully feminine and extremely melodious, when exercised in what is termed level speaking. Its powers seem not yet to have arrived at sufficient maturity to accommodate themselves adequately to the more violent exertions of the violent passions. Her countenance is agreeable, and her features regular and tolerably expressive; happily so, where the situation demands a smile. She speaks naturally, and lays her accent and the emphasis with critical correctness. Her performance was interesting, and fairly entitled to great commendation.[38]

In addition to her native ability and youthful appeal, Anne was supported by a strong cast headed by one of London's finest actors, John Henderson, whose portrayal that night was unusually brilliant. Some even suggested that he overshadowed the young lady.[39] Ill at the time, he so exerted himself in the third act that afterward he required a considerable time to recover in the green room.[40] Unfortunately Anne played opposite Henderson only three more times before he died the following month. At the time, he was London's reigning tragic actor, fame that John Kemble assumed only after Henderson's death. His most acclaimed portrayals suggested an amazing breadth of ability: Richard III, Hamlet, Lear, Iago, Falstaff, Shylock, Benedick, and Malvolio. Praised for his correct reading of lines, Henderson was also noted for his ability to identify with his character, for his keen powers of concentration, and, in contrast to Kemble, for his spontaneity in the expression of emotion. It is impossible to know how much Henderson influenced Anne Brunton's acting. However it is interesting to note that both Henderson and Anne had been described as "chaste" players—"very little action . . . no tricks of

---

[37] Dunlap, *History of the American Theatre*, I, 337; Boaden, *Memoirs of John Philip Kemble*, I, 293.
[38] *European Magazine*, VIII (September, 1785), 307.
[39] Haslewood, *The Secret History of the Green-Room*, II, 88.
[40] London *Daily Universal Register*, October 19, 1785.

voice"—and that both were noted for their intense identification with characterizations and the correct reading of lines.[41]

As the novelty of the fall theatre season, Anne drew large and fashionable audiences. Her third performance of *The Roman Father* attracted many of the nobility, including the Prince of Wales and the Duke of Cumberland. Their entrance into the king's box excited extra flurry and delay as his Royal Highness acknowledged the applause of the audience with repeated bows.[42]

Several distinguished persons in a full house were again on hand when Anne performed Euphrasia for the first time in London. No doubt many came in order to compare the youthful actress with Mrs. Siddons, who had played the same role as recently as the Saturday prior to Anne's debut. Acknowledging the fact that he was avoiding "invidious comparison," the critic for the *Daily Universal Register* praised the performance and noted Anne's ability to express violent and tender emotions. But he also pointed out that the young actress was unable to maintain sufficient majestic bearing.[43] The same writer, critical of John Brunton's performance, advised him against playing Anne's stage father again because his own tender feelings toward his child affected his believability. Whether these specific comments prompted Brunton to relinquish the role is not known, but when John Henderson took over the part in the next performance the reviewer complimented Brunton for respecting public opinion. In the meantime Anne's characterizations grew stronger as her performances increased in number. By the time of her fifth representation of Euphrasia in January, she was winning extended applause and receiving commendation for improvement in grace and enunciation.[44]

The third role Anne Brunton created that season was Juliet (*Romeo and Juliet*), perhaps the most significant in her first year, for as she developed her art, Juliet became her most acclaimed

[41] Bertram Joseph, *The Tragic Actor* (London, 1959), 177–86.
[42] London *Daily Universal Register*, October 25, 1785.
[43] *Ibid.*, October 29, 1785.
[44] *Ibid.*, November 1, 1785; January 17, 1786.

role. Her early performances, however, drew censure: one critic objected to her declamatory delivery, while another writer recognized that the young girl did not have the emotional depths to comprehend Juliet's feelings nor a sufficiently mobile face to reveal the emotions. Comment was made that her scene beginning "Now I am alone" lacked animation, but in her final tomb scene she was especially moving when she upbraided the friar in tones of resentment and despair.[45] At sixteen, with perhaps no more than twenty performances and three roles to her credit, the young woman was not ready to handle the full scope of the demanding role. Other theatre critics would undoubtedly concur with Boaden that if she had the youthful simplicity and ardor of the early scenes, it was nearly impossible for her to possess the maturity and skill required in the later scenes.[46]

The same weakness was observed in her next characterization of Monimia, in Thomas Otway's blank verse tragedy *The Orphan*. Although Mrs. Siddons frequently performed Belvidera in Otway's other popular tragedy *Venice Preserv'd*, she declined to play Monimia.[47] She may have realized that she was unsuited to the pathetic role or she may have disliked the play. Because the role was not the acclaimed property of Mrs. Siddons, Covent Garden manager Thomas Harris apparently attempted to establish Anne in the part of the wronged and pathetic Monimia who is deceived into sharing her bridal bed with the brother of her bridegroom. Appearing in a dress of white satin, much admired by the audience, she was praised for the scenes with Polydore where pride is the operating passion and for those in the last two acts, in which Monimia expresses amazement, horror, and despair.[48] One critic's suggestion that she "modulate her voice more and free herself from the disagreeable jerk of the body," indicates that her voice and body were not always under control.[49] In spite of such criticism, Anne won sufficient approval to schedule both Monimia

---

[45] *Ibid.*, November 15, 1785.
[46] Boaden, *Memoirs of John Philip Kemble*, I, 299.
[47] London *Daily Universal Register*, December 2, 1785.
[48] *Ibid.*, December 8, 1785.
[49] *Ibid.*

and Juliet more than any other roles in her first London season, playing each nine times.

The first role Anne learned in the new year was Hermione in *The Distressed Mother,* a reworking of Racine's *Andromaque.* Although Hermione was acknowledged as a difficult role, Anne's performance was judged to be marvelous. Nevertheless the drama played only three times that season, perhaps because "Miss Brunton's figure and youth were too insignificant for Hermione," or perhaps because in Mrs. Wells's performance of Andromache she displayed "beauty without grace—or grief without feeling."[50]

Although the atmosphere of the great patent theatre must have been exciting for Anne during that first year, one event must have been especially memorable for her. On February 25 Mrs. Siddons added lustre to Covent Garden history by appearing there in one of her most famous roles, Belvidera (*Venice Preserv'd*), for the benefit of John Henderson's widow. For the event the pit was converted into boxes. One might well imagine the neophyte's emotions as she witnessed the great actress' performance.

In March, Anne attempted her second Shakespearean role, Cordelia, in *King Lear.* Although her characterization was pronounced "chaste, yet animated" and Cordelia later became a staple in her repertoire, the tragedy was mounted only once that season, perhaps because the cast lacked the stability of Henderson's Lear. On March 14 the young actress enjoyed the honor of one of the first benefit performances of the season, a theatrical custom which gave an actor the evening's box office receipts after expenses were deducted. For the occasion John Brunton selected *Werter,* adapted by Frederick Reynolds from Goethe's popular romantic novella concerning the desperate young man who commits suicide over his unrequited love for his friend's honorable wife Charlotte. The work had already achieved some success at its première in Bath the previous December: the nervous young playwright Reynolds, peeping through a hole in the green curtain

---

[50] *Ibid.,* February 2, 1786.

before the performance, had seen white handkerchiefs spread on the front of boxes in imitation of a ceremony regularly performed when Mrs. Siddons played.[51] By the conclusion of the first scene between Charlotte and Werter, the busy handkerchiefs were interpreted by the greenroom as a strong indication of approval. In subsequent acts the scent of hartshorn and the fainting of four ladies announced success! Equal, if not superior success, accompanied the London performance. In addition to the obvious appeal of the pathetic situation presented in Werter, Reynolds attributed the play's favorable reception to London theatregoers' determination not to be outdone by the provincials, and to the popularity of George Holman and Anne Brunton, who performed the play four times that spring.[52]

Before the season ended, Anne played three other characterizations. In addition to Palmira (Mahomet), she attempted sentimental comedy for the first time when she performed in Edward Moore's The Foundling as Fidelia, a young woman whose goodness converts her libertine lover. Although she performed the role only one more time that spring, the characterization helped to establish her versatility.[53]

The last part Anne learned in her opening season at Covent Garden was that of Zara in William Congreve's gloomy Restoration "thriller" The Mourning Bride. No doubt she was unsuited in age and temperament to depict a captive princess who reveals the rage of a scorned woman, inconsolable grief, and violence which leads to suicide. In future years Anne often played the other important female role, the gentle, long-suffering Almeria, a part which seems more appropriate for her.

A second performance of The Mourning Bride was Anne's last before returning to Bath and Bristol, where she was featured in The Grecian Daughter, The Distressed Mother, and Romeo and

[51] Frederick Reynolds, The Life and Times of Frederick Reynolds written by Himself (London, 1827), I, 305.
[52] Ibid., 315.
[53] London Daily Universal Register, April 10, 1786.

Juliet. The latter, a benefit performance, earned her the sum of £130, indicating that she had not been forgotten in her year's absence from Bath.

During Anne's first season in London she played eleven roles in forty–seven performances, a substantial schedule for a beginning actress. The kinds of roles she played suggest that the manager attempted to identify her with spirited and animated characterizations as well as with those requiring tender and violent emotions. Although eighteenth century tragedies dominated her repertoire, her most frequently performed roles were Shakespeare's Juliet and Otway's Monimia. Her debut vehicles, *The Roman Father* and *The Grecian Daughter*, were scheduled almost as often, each seven times.

Throughout her first season at Covent Garden, Anne drew audiences described as brilliant and overflowing. They came to be astonished by the sixteen-year-old's melodious voice, her easy and graceful body movement, commanding stage presence, and touching revelation of gentle emotions. Although the public endorsed the young actress with enthusiastic attendance, the critics were cautious. Most of them agreed that she was talented and showed great promise, but they also pointed out that because of youthfulness and inexperience, she lacked the emotional depth and technical skill for fully developed characterizations. In predicting her future success, James Boaden concluded, "yet study will always do something, and she seemed a refined and sensible actress."[54] Only time itself would reveal whether she would fulfill the promise of her "early excellence."

[54] Boaden, *Memoirs of John Philip Kemble*, I, 299.

II
In the British Isles
1786-1796

The initial clamor that Anne Brunton created during the season of 1785–1786 at Covent Garden reverberated through the provinces, making her a desirable acquisition for provincial managers eager to assemble attractive summer companies. Because both of the main patent London theatres were closed during the summer, provincial managers were able to hire leading London actors who sought limited seasonal employment in the provincial theatres of England, Scotland, and Ireland. Although many actors remained in London, accepting employment at pleasure gardens, minor theatres, or the Haymarket (the only patent summer theatre), many contracted for lucrative provincial summer engagements. By February 20, 1786, Anne had negotiated for a challenging summer schedule. Her itinerary included eight nights each at Norwich, Birmingham, and Liverpool, and two weeks in Cork, Ireland.[1]

Cork newspapers report that Anne performed the popular roles from her previous London season; Euphrasia, Monimia, Hermione, and Horatia.[2] Again she fascinated audiences with her melodious voice and expressive eyes; even the antics of two competing London comedians, John Henry Johnston and Charles Bannister, did not eclipse her performances.

The demanding summer schedule provided her the opportunity to develop consistency and control in performance, essential

---

[1] London *Daily Universal Register*, February 20, 1786.
[2] William Smith Clark, *The Irish Stage in the County Towns, 1720 to 1800* (Oxford, 1965), 124.

skills attainable through the discipline of practical stage experience. When she returned to London, the value of the summer
tour seemed evident to at least one critic, who acknowledged
that "the Brunton has improved considerably from last season."[3]

Although she may now have been a better actress, turnover in
the Covent Garden company placed her in a less advantageous
position than the previous season. Mrs. Pope, who rejoined her
husband on Covent Garden boards after a year's absence, was the
most significant change. In addition to the advantages of approximately twenty–five years seniority, in age and experience, Mrs.
Pope's versatile powers allowed her to take over both comic and
tragic roles which otherwise might have fallen to the fledgling
actress.

For her first appearance of the season, Anne returned to her
well-established role, Euphrasia in *The Grecian Daughter*, performing for the first time with a Covent Garden newcomer, William McCready, known at the time as a "second-rate Walking
Gentleman" and later as the father of the famous nineteenth
century tragedian.[4] Far more significant for Anne that fall was her
first new role of the season, Alicia, in Nicholas Rowe's forerunner
to domestic tragedy, *Jane Shore*. The drama, which demands
strong representations in both leading female roles, concerns the
fate of Jane Shore, a former royal mistress. After her fall from
court favor Lord Hastings comes to her aid; he also attempts to
force his attentions on her but is prevented by Jane's protectors,
Dumont and Belmour. Hastings' fortunes take a turn for the worse
when his former lover Alicia betrays him after discovering his new
love for Jane Shore. The betrayal leads to Hastings' execution
and Jane's being turned into the streets. When the forsaken
woman seeks help, Alicia's callous determination not to aid her
former rival leads to her own mental breakdown and Jane Shore's
total collapse. However, before she dies Jane receives the forgive-
ness of her husband Shore, who has been disguised as Belmour.

With Mrs. Pope playing the title role, the tragedy gave play-

[3] London *Daily Universal Register*, October 4, 1786.
[4] Haslewood, *The Secret History of the Green-Room*, I, 285.

goers an opportunity to see the neophyte and the experienced actress together. Among the curious was Mrs. Siddons, who often portrayed the title role at Drury Lane. She gave visible approval of the Covent Garden production with applause and with tears during the fifth act's final tender scene between Shore and his wife.[5]

Although Anne "added to her reputation" in her portrayal of Alicia's impassioned rage and insanity, her parting scene with Hastings lacked tenderness.[6] Understandably her youthfulness continued to be a compromising factor. Some critics believed that she was "being pushed into characters above her powers. The part of Alicia requires the well-matured genius and exertions of the first actress of the Stage." Such criticism may have motivated Anne to greater effort, for a second performance revealed an improved Alicia "both in force and discrimination." Nevertheless the combined ability of the two leading ladies could not sustain *Jane Shore* beyond one more performance that season. And on that occasion the gallery audience endured it as a long preface to the new pantomine *The Enchanted Castle*.[7]

Along with portraying Alicia and repeating successes of the previous season such as Horatia, Juliet, Monimia, Zara, and Charlotte, Anne undertook the famous role of Calista in Rowe's other outstanding success *The Fair Penitent* (based on Massinger's *The Fatal Dowry*). This production, popular for its virtuoso performances and pathetic domestic situations, depicts the tragic fate of Calista, victim of a faithless lover, Lothario, with whom she has an affair before her marriage to Altamont. Calista frantically denies her past, but Altamont eventually learns the truth, whereupon Calista commits suicide. Although Anne convincingly portrayed "the hauteur, the refinement—and the disdain of Calista" and was commended for omitting those passages of level speaking "unsuited to her voice," in other respects her perfor-

[5] London *Daily Universal Register*, October 4, 9, 1786.
[6] *Ibid.*, October 7, 1786.
[7] *European Magazine*, X (October, 1786), 297; London *Daily Universal Register*, October 14, December 27, 1786.

mance was disappointing. Her weaknesses, delineated by critics, suggest that she still was not mature enough to comprehend the role. In the first scene, for instance, "her despondence and conscious humiliation were well expressed; but when she talked of an asylum, where to hide her sorrows and her shame, instead of the blushing anguish that should accompany the latter, Miss Brunton seemed to glory in proclaiming it to the audience." Her inadequacies may have caused the "riotous spirit" which became so tumultuous that the performance was "frequently suspended for several minutes and in no part of the conclusion was the attention of the decent part of the audience suffered to be entirely undisturbed."[8] The play received only one more performance that season and scant attention from Anne until she matured in age and experience in her art.

In December, Frederick Reynolds offered Covent Garden his second tragedy, *Eloisa* (based on Rousseau's novel by the same name), and Anne her first opportunity to originate a role. Unfortunately the production had only three performances, in spite of an opening night claque of more than one hundred Westminster boys who rushed into the boxes and pit "determined . . . to support the production of a brother Westminster." Reynolds' mother also had scattered at least fifty young men "to maintain a proper circulation of the applause through all parts of the house." As painfully tangible testimony to the failure of the work, Reynolds' benefit exceeded the £100 house expenses by only £8.[9] Anne's only consolation may have been praise of her ability to enter "very deeply into the conflicting passions of Eloisa; her indignation, her rage, and her disdain, had all the usual force; but were also recommended by a very happy, and judicious discrimination."[10]

The young actress did not present another new role until her benefit in April, when she made her first appearance in Shakespearean comedy as Beatrice in *Much Ado About Nothing*. News-

8 London *Daily Universal Register*, November 28, 1786.
9 Reynolds, *The Life of Frederick Reynolds*, I, 321–22, 323.
10 London *Daily Universal Register*, December 21, 1786.

papers announced that tickets could be had from Miss Brunton herself at No. 5 George–street, York-buildings. Even though she earned a respectable £220 from the performance, this response did not encourage the repetition of her Beatrice. She played one other Shakespearean role that spring, Perdita, in *The Winter's Tale*, while her last new role of the season was Cecelia, the heroine in Sophia Lee's climax to sentimental comedy, *The Chapter of Accidents*.

In her second season at Covent Garden, Anne gave twenty-nine performances of fourteen roles, seven of them new, a disappointing record compared to the previous season when she gave forty-six performances in ten roles. A published account of the Covent Garden Theatrical Benefits for the year, arranged in the order in which they took place, indicates her fall in popularity:

Mrs. Billington	£270	Mr. Quick	£321
Mrs. Pope	290	Mrs. Mattocks	220
Mr. Ryder	260	Mr. Aickin	180
Mr. Lewis	300	Mr. Leoni	280
Mr. Edwin	320	Mrs. Martyr	300
Miss Brunton	220	Mr. Farren	300
Mr. Holman	300	Mr. Pope	200[11]

No doubt Mrs. Pope's return affected the number of Anne's appearances as well as her popularity. Having begun her long acting career under the tutelege of David Garrick, Mrs. Pope had the advantages of age, experience, and versatility. As a leading actress at Drury Lane and later at Covent Garden, she was an invaluable asset to managers, who could count on her excellence in both tragic and comic roles. It was generally acknowledged that she could not excel Sarah Siddons in tragedy or Elizabeth Farren in comedy, but nevertheless she had a wider range than either. In the course of her career, her tragic roles extended from Lady Macbeth to Juliet and her comic from Rosalind to chambermaids. Probably the greatest testimonial to Mrs. Pope's versatility came from manager Thomas Harris, who at the time of her death

[11] *Ibid.*, April 30, 1787. Slightly different figures for these benefits appear in Hogan (ed.), *The London Stage*, 949–71.

lamented that "the greatest loss he could ever sustain had just befallen him."[12] Anne Brunton was seldom directly compared with Mrs. Pope, although as she matured, the younger actress seemed to develop a comparable range. A difference in age and ability probably divided the leading Covent Garden dramatic roles between them; Mrs. Pope often portrayed Lady Macbeth, Portia, and Rosalind, whereas Anne became identified with the younger, gentler characters such as Juliet and Cordelia. Mrs. Pope's reappearance at Covent Garden had the advantage of relieving Anne from attempting roles she was not ready for in age or experience. Thus, in the long run, the two actresses served as complements to one another rather than as competitors. But during the first year in which they performed together, Mrs. Pope was undoubtedly a threat to the younger actress.

At the same time, Anne's reviews indicate the unwillingness of critics to tolerate her inadequacies because of her youthfulness. After witnessing a performance of *The Grecian Daughter* early in the season, one writer declared that her deficiencies "remain unabated; her emphasis was thrown out as usual by starts; her voice is still the same, its tones frequently strike with pleasure on the ear, but its melody in many passages seem [*sic*] too much the effect of study, and frequently impedes articulation." Throughout the season her delivery drew criticism. Here "strong breathing with which she fills every interval in her tragical declamation . . . destroys the illusion of the scene," possibly calling attention to the artist at work. She was also criticized for lifting "her voice so much above its natural tone, that the cadence is lost . . . . This may be easily corrected; but if too much indulged, she will gradually acquire a bad habit of ranting, and instead of expressing passion, tear it into rags." Still another weakness in the second season was her "apparent want of feeling," particularly noted in a performance of Horatia.[13] While her delivery and lack of feeling were criticized often enough in her first two years to establish

---

[12] Boaden, *Memoirs of John Philip Kemble*, I, 87.
[13] London *Daily Universal Register*, September 27, October 17, 1786; May 31, 1787; October 23, 1786.

them as undisputed weaknesses, Anne also received sufficient praise to indicate that she had frequently given effective performances. As Charlotte, for example, her "*look* and agitation during Werter's *readings,* with the subsequent exclamations of *Werter!* *Werter!!* *Werter!!!* cannot be exceeded by the *Siddons!*"[14] She may have had difficulty maintaining her effectiveness, however, when George Holman, playing the desperate Werter, struck his head so hard that the Mareschale powder flew from his wig in great quantities. She also received commendations for her performance of Juliet as "excellent and chaste" and "altogether superior." Most noteworthy was the garden scene with Romeo, "especially as . . . her private conduct is such, as would grace a woman of superior rank, which to those who are acquainted with her character, renders the pathetic part of her acting doubly interesting."[15] This commendation of her private character is one of the first of many similar comments throughout her life, testifying to her personal integrity.

In the light of dimming enthusiasm, as well as the general disenchantment with the child wonder, her future success may have seemed highly questionable. However Anne interpreted the situation, she did not hesitate to accept summer engagements in Ireland.[16] During a three-weeks stay in Belfast, she depended on her established characterizations: Horatia, Euphrasia, Calista, Beatrice, Juliet, and Monima. She also performed Perdita in *Florizel and Perdita,* Garrick's adaptation of Shakespeare's *Winter's Tale.* There, too, she made her first and perhaps only attempt at comic opera in the title role of Frances Brooke's *Rosina.* Belfast audiences appreciated her for the same qualities recognized in London, "her rare sweetness of modulation, expressive face, and elegant taste in dress." She was also compared favorably with Mrs. Siddons who had captivated Belfast the summer before. "In tenderness of look and mild intonations the towering talent of Mrs. Siddons falls short of Excellence, whereas Miss Brunton

[14] *Ibid.* October 29, 1786.
[15] *Ibid.,* December 13, 1786.
[16] Clark, *The Irish Stage,* 262–63.

excels, tho' she does not attempt so bold a flight."[17] In spite of approval from the local critic, she did not draw large audiences; this must have been discouraging, but may have renewed her determination as she returned to her third London season.

A series of unsuccessful new presentations and revivals but a remarkably profitable box office characterized the 1787–1788 Covent Garden season. The fortunes of the theatre and Anne's career were analogous. Like the theatre she experienced several unsuccessful performances, but also like the theatre season, her performances were generally praised. Nevertheless the season must have been disheartening, for in total number of performances she played no more than the previous year. Moreover the only role which demanded as many as four performances was Statira in Nathaniel Lee's *Alexander The Great*. The favorable comments which she earned for her portrayal of Alexander's wronged wife were typical for the entire year: "Miss Brunton was everything in Statira that criticism could wish—her resentment—jealousy—returning love—were all finely marked."[18] The same production introduced the young actress to the brilliant and talented gentleman-actor James Fennell, whose career crossed hers in London as well as the United States. Playing the title role of Alexander, Fennell appeared at Covent Garden under the assumed name of Cambray. Later he joined the ranks of professional actors in England, Scotland, and America; but in the fall of 1787 he created a considerable attraction as an amateur in such roles as Alexander, Othello, Jaffier, and Macbeth.

Perhaps the most significant aspect of Anne's third year was her successful initiation into the realm of sentimental comedy after rather tentative attempts the previous year. Typical laudatory remarks appeared following her first performance as Indiana in Richard Steele's early sentimental comedy *The Conscious Lovers*. The critic praised her "delicate colouring" of emotions and a "thorough knowledge of her author."[19] Perhaps such en-

17 *Ibid.*, Clark cites the Belfast *News-Letter*.
18 London *Daily Universal Register*, October 23, 1787.
19 London *Times*, February 5, 1788. The *Daily Universal Register* became the *Times* beginning January 2, 1788.

dorsement encouraged the selection of another sentimental heroine, Julia in Sheridan's *The Rivals*, for her benefit on March 28,
1788. That performance "added greatly to her theatrical fame,"
especially the scene with Faulkland "where he represents the
consequences of the feigned duel, she evinced a sensibility of soul,
beyond which acting could not go:—and her subsequent resentment on discovering his duplicity, claimed equal approbation."[20]

With this addition of sentimental comedy, Anne's increased
versatility conformed to the managerial emphasis of the playhouse. Following John Henderson's death, the Drury Lane company headed by Mrs. Siddons had definitely assumed supremacy
in tragedy. While the comic strength of the two patent houses
seems to have been equal that year, Harris obviously hoped to tip
the balance in favor of Covent Garden by bringing out a number
of new comedies and after-pieces.

While she expanded her repertoire, Anne established herself
in roles portraying the ladylike heroines of sentimental comedy,
rather than in the more broadly humorous comic parts depicting
boisterous and saucy serving maids. As Boaden pointed out, seldom was one actress adept at both lines of comic business: "the
perfect representation of refinement and vulgarity never belongs
to one actress. The domestics of Mrs. Abington had too much of
the lady. The fashionable women of Mrs. Jordan had always some
tang of the country girl."[21] Anne's "melodious voice," "tenderness
of look and mild intonations," and "delicate colouring" of emotions ideally suited the portrayal of sentimental heroines expressing refined sentiments while enduring hardships from which they
are successfully rescued. This new line of acting broadened the
scope of her repertoire and enlarged her technical range. Fur-
thermore it may well have been the turning point in her acting
career, establishing her as a more versatile actress and in an area
in which many, later, considered her unrivalled.

Nevertheless Anne apparently did not believe the year had been
generally profitable, for as early as March 18 she refused to renew

[20] *Ibid.*, April 10, 1788.
[21] Boaden, *Memoirs of John Philip Kemble*, I, 391.

her contract with Covent Garden and made plans to join a company in a "sister kingdom."[22] Specific motivations for her decision are not known. Perhaps a season which saw no improvement in the total number of performances over the previous year tempted the actress to seek a management which would assure her of more opportunities to act and perhaps more money. Whatever her reservations about renewing her articles of agreement with Harris, they persisted at least until May 19 when the *Times* announced that she had changed her mind and had accepted a Covent Garden engagement for three more years, with a salary increase from £6 to £8 weekly.

During the same spring, her father was negotiating for the Norwich Theatre management, which he assumed the following summer. In spite of her father's new position, Anne did not become part of his summer company. Instead she opened at the Birmingham theatre in June, with an established role from her repertoire, Horatia, in *The Roman Father*.[23] She also scheduled summer appearances in Manchester and other provincial theatres. Her departure for the provinces was marked by a summary note in the *Times* which prophesied that Anne Brunton promised "one day to be high in the line of her profession. Had she the person equal to Mrs. Siddons, she would soon dispute the palm of victory with that great lady;—but if nature has been niggard in that respect, she has been bountiful in others."[24] However flattering it was to be compared with Mrs. Siddons, Anne must have yearned to be recognized as more than a "promise" or a shorter version of the older artist.

Simultaneously the nineteen-year-old actress must have begun to feel somewhat like a veteran performer by the fall of 1788, as she returned from her third summer in the provinces to a new three-year engagement at Covent Garden. The reception of her opening performance as Juliet must have been particularly gratifying, for it "was marked with all that warmth of applause which

[22] London *Times*, March 18, 1788.
[23] *Ibid.*, May 20, June 11, 1788.
[24] *Ibid.*, June 12, 1788.

the public ever bestows on its favourites." Her portrayal of Leonora in Edward Young's *The Revenge* soon after identified her
as one "who hourly gains upon the public," while she revealed
"evident signs of improvement" as the "love sick tender Monimia."[25] In November her popularity reached new heights in her
creation of Amanthis, from Mrs. Inchbald's adaptation of a
French piece entitled *The Child of Nature*. The title role, which
soon became synonymous with Anne, ideally suited her age and
emphasized her personal charm. Originally played in five acts
and gradually pruned to two, the comedy deals with the romance
of a Count Valentia and his lovely young ward Amanthis. Fearful
that his charge will be ruined by the contamination of the world,
the count rears her within his own castle, personally supervising
her education. When she emerges at seventeen as a lovely young
woman, the count discovers he is hopelessly in love with her but
mistakenly interprets her innocent, warm response to him as mere
gratitude. The inevitable union of the couple is delayed, first, by
a libertine suitor who misinterprets Amanthis' reactions as en-
couragements and, second, by the return of her long-lost father
who tests her filial love. Eventually the count wins his Child of
Nature as his wife. Described as an "elegant trifle," the comedy
owed its great popularity to the novel portrayal of simple, unaf-
fected innocence by "Miss *Brunton*—who, by every look, word,
and action, proved herself a genuine CHILD OF NATURE"; the
comedy itself, however, was unable to "exist without the most
powerful support."[26] The managers were forced to bill it with
other short plays or as an after-piece, but the twenty-four performances of the comedy that season clearly attest to Anne's stage
magnetism. Most of these appearances occurred before February,
when the management introduced another success, O'Keeffe's
The Toy, which provided Anne ten more performances that
spring.

The last and most significant of the three roles Anne originated during the season of 1788–1789 was Louisa Courtney in

[25] *Ibid.*, September, 23, October 4, 28, 1788.
[26] *Ibid.*, November 29, December 10, 1788.

The Dramatist, Frederick Reynolds' first attempt at comedy. Written to display the comic powers of William Lewis, the amiable acting-manager of Covent Garden, the comedy was grudgingly mounted by actors convinced (Lewis, most of all) that it would fail.[27] In spite of Lewis' dislike for his role of Vapid, the "Dramatist," he "played with such skill, spirit, and enthusiasm, that, when he rushed out of a china closet, in the fourth act, the roars of laughter were immense, and his triumph was complete." Having opened in April, the comedy did not reach its greatest popularity until the following season when *The Dramatist* played "with success never equalled" in Boaden's memory. Anne rode the crest of the work's popularity, fulfilling the part of the young heroine with "everything the author could wish, lively, delicate, and interesting."[28] The comedy seems to have been a significant factor in changing the destiny of several persons involved in its original production. For Lewis it provided a comic tour de force for the rest of his career, and for the author it pointed to a dramatic form best suited to his talents. For Anne it may have served as an introduction to the writer of its prologue Robert Merry, who eventually became her husband and a prime influence in changing the course of her career.

One other noteworthy event occurred that spring. On May 7 Charles Macklin made his last appearance in his famous portrayal of Shylock. At the time, he claimed to be about ninety years old, although some believed he was older. For several years Macklin had been making sporadic appearances at Covent Garden, but in 1788 he gave evidence of not being able to remember his lines. On the evening of his last appearance the management anticipated his inability to finish the performance, and after several incoherent speeches the old actor, begging the audience's pardon, gracefully turned over his role to a fellow actor.[29] Only a year before, Macklin was still writing plays and anticipating their pro-

[27] Reynolds, *The Life of Frederick Reynolds*, II, 32.

[28] *Ibid.*; Boaden, *Memoirs of John Philip Kemble*, II, 13; London *Times*, May 25, 1789.

[29] Genest, *Some Account of the British Stage*, VI, 556–57.

duction. In one of them he intended Mrs. Pope as the heroine, "which is the character of the perfect female—not a seduced one."[30] Mrs. Pope somehow fell from his favor and Anne Brunton became his ideal for the heroine. Unfortunately the play never saw production.

The Covent Garden curtain came down June 18, 1789, on a season successful for the playhouse and for Anne, who played sixty-three performances, a significant increase over the year before when she appeared only twenty-nine times. Of her seven new roles, six were comic. With a total of forty-four performances in comedy, compared to nineteen in tragedies, comedy definitely assumed the lead in her repertoire.

Largely because of the success of *The Dramatist*, comedy continued to command most of Anne's energies in the following season. During 1789–1790, the busiest season of her entire British career, she appeared seventy-three times in eighteen roles, originating eight new ones. Of her fifty-two appearances in comedies, at least thirty-four were as Louisa in Reynolds' comic hit. Eleven of the other seventeen roles were performed only once. The lopsided statistics indicate an unusual season. Drury Lane was not offering its usual threat in the area of tragedy, because Mrs. Siddons did not perform in London during that season nor until late in the next one. Her absence seemed to invite aspirants to usurp her vacant throne. Manager Harris met the opportunity with a beautiful new Juliet, Catherine Ann Achmet from Dublin. The newcomer won several roles during the season, but critics resented her assumption of the role of Juliet, which had become identified with Anne Brunton.[31] In spite of her beauty, Mrs. Achmet did not win a second year's engagement and she returned to Dublin without seriously threatening Anne's position at Covent Garden.[32] Harris made other attempts to capture the lovers of tragedy: George Holman (after a two-year absence) and Mrs. Pope performed *Macbeth*; James Fennell appeared as Othello,

[30] London *Times*, March 26, 1788.
[31] *Ibid.*, September 23, 1789.
[32] Haslewood, *The Secret History of the Green-Room*, II, 162.

Hotspur, and Edmund (*King Lear*); and, Harley, from Norwich, was introduced as Richard III, with Anne making her first appearance as Lady Anne. But without the electrifying appearances of Mrs. Siddons it became clear that "this . . . [was] not the season for tragedies."[33]

To satisfy comic appetites the manager revived traditionally staple attractions such as *The Beaux' Stratagem, The Conscious Lovers, The Constant Couple, The Merchant of Venice, As You Like It,* and (after a sixteen-year absence) a revival of *The Clandestine Marriage.* Regardless of such offerings, the *Times* complained that "Covent Garden Theatre has produced nothing yet this season which has not been disapproved. . . . No wonder that the House cuts such a gloomy appearance every night till such time as the half-price loungers come and molest the Theatre with a riot."[34] Undoubtedly Harris was thankful that the popularity of *The Dramatist* could help counteract the rejection of other offerings.

While the season of 1789–1790 provided Anne with many opportunities to play a number of roles, it did not afford any new turn in her dramatic career. The only noteworthy new part she attempted the entire season was Penelope in Garrick's adaptation of *The Gamester* by James Shirley. The role demands sophisticated "archness" in the feminine lead, a quality usually not required of actresses performing sentimental "fine ladies." Anne played the role so successfully that the newspaper congratulated her "on finding her way so completely through a path of drama perfectly new to this charming young actress. Her first opening with *Wilding,* and her last aclairissement with *Hazard* . . . were very near equal in archness and effect to the best we have witnessed. . . .Whilst Miss *Brunton* continues to take *nature* as her guide she has not anything to fear—for she must succeed."[35] Although the season did not challenge Anne with any other significant new roles, perhaps this year, more than any other in her

[33] London *Times*, December 15, 1789.
[34] *Ibid.*, December 8, 1789.
[35] *Ibid.*, January 23, 1790.

early career, tested her stamina to withstand the exhausting demands of the repertory system, especially when rejection of new plays required the hasty resurrection of substitutions. Between September and January she learned three new roles, revived seven other parts, and performed in *The Dramatist* eleven times.

Records do not reveal whether Anne followed the strenuous year of performing with a visit with her family in Norwich or with summer engagements, but in the fall of 1790–1791 "very cordial applause" greeted her and George Holman when they opened the Covent Garden season with *Romeo and Juliet*.[36] "There was no novelty" in the performance, and the large audience was "ascribed to the attraction of the old performers." During the course of the season, the management offered London a series of favorites from previous seasons and a new leading lady who provided a fresh challenge to Anne's status at Covent Garden. The newcomer, Harriet Pye Esten, had enjoyed acclaim at Bath and Edinburgh but had never won a Covent Garden contract. However, in the fall of 1790 Harris allowed her a trial engagement without salary but with the "indulgence of appearing in whatever character she chose." Mrs. Esten's initial appearance as Rosalind in *As You Like It* earned such approval that the manager hoped "she would draw crowds during the season."[37] Two days after her first success, the attractive actress asserted her versatility in a double bill; she performed Indiana in *The Conscious Lovers* and Roxalana in *The Sultan*. The bill was demanding and daring because it invited comparison with Anne's successful portrayal of Indiana and Dorothy Jordan's noted excellence as Roxalana at Drury Lane. The challenge did not aid Mrs. Esten's reputation; but, at the same time, she did not suffer by the comparison with the established actresses: ". . . in either [part] we cannot think she by any means surpassed her contemporaries, Miss *Brunton* and Mrs. *Jordan*—Still both were performed in so creditable style, as almost fully to justify the applause with which they were accompanied." Mrs. Esten contin-

---

[36] *European Magazine*, XVIII (September, 1790), 221.
[37] *Ibid.*; Haslewood, *The Secret History of the Green-Room*, II, 133, 132.

ued to enact characters in which Anne as well as leading ladies of Drury Lane were most admired. Although "her performances were much above mediocrity," she never overshadowed the leading attractions of the two patent houses, and on some occasions the press openly lamented the "absence of that truest Actress— Dame NATURE!" Nevertheless in one instance the *Times* suggested that Anne relinquish a role to the newcomer, after a performance of Dryden's *All for Love*, because "Miss *Brunton*, with all her delicacy and beauty, unhappily affords not the smallest trait of 'Cleopatra's MAJESTY.' "[38] No doubt the criticism was well founded, for Cleopatra never became an active characterization in Anne's repertoire, and her lack of majestic bearing plagued and limited the scope of her tragic range in the early part of her career.

Of the new productions offered during the season, the most significant for Anne was a pantomime, *The Picture of Paris, Taken in the Year of* 1790. Although she performed in it only twice, the pantomime is a signal event in her career for it undoubtedly brought her in contact with its author Robert Merry, her future husband.[39] Because Anne seldom performed in after-pieces, her appearance in the pantomime suggests that manager Harris employed all available acting talent to insure the production's success. He also allowed expenditures for "entirely new scenery, machinery and decorations," prepared by five artists "with many Assistants." The several scenes in the work, "taken from accurate Drawings on the Spot," included The Inside of the Hotel de Ville, The Fountain of Innocence, A Grand Assembly, and A View of the Triumphal Arch, all of which were "intended to be a representation of various scenes that were exhibited during the revolution in France." The listing suggests the political nature of the subject matter, certain to raise the English Tory eyebrows of a jittery Pitt government worried that the Revolution would

[38] London *Times*, October 25, 1790; Haslewood, *The Secret History of the Green-Room*, II, 123; London *Times*, October 28, November 2, 1790.
[39] Dougald Macmillan (comp.), *Catalogue of the Larpent Plays in the Huntington Library* (San Marino, 1939), no. 886. Charles Bonner as well as Merry is listed as author.

spread to England. Significantly, critical comments on the day following its opening suggested that the theatre "ought ever to steer clear of politics."[40] Even at the risk of censorship from the Lord Chamberlain's office, Harris probably hoped to capitalize on current topical subject matter. The pantomime may have seemed an especially good risk moreover because its author had won pronounced success as the poet Della Crusca. With this attempt to capture holiday audiences, Harris inadvertently created another turning point in the career of Anne Brunton, who soon fell in love with the poet, playwright, and politician Robert Merry.

Born in 1755 in London of an aristocratic family, the poet was a descendant of Sir Henry Merry, knighted by James I at Whitehall in 1621.[41] His family's interest in the North American continent began with Robert Merry's grandfather, a captain in the royal navy, who discovered the island in the North Seas which became identified as Merry's Island; he also helped establish the commercial plans of the Hudson's Bay Company. Captain Merry's adventuresome spirit led him to make a voyage to the East Indies, returning overland to England on a journey reputedly filled with hardships. Captain Merry's son became governor of the Hudson's Bay Company and married Margaret Willes, eldest daughter of Lord Chief Justice, Sir John Willes. Their first child was Robert, whose education became the trust of his father's sister.[42] As a young man, Merry attended Harrow under the tutelage of the celebrated liberal thinker Dr. Samuel Parr. While a taste for adventure might well have been a family trait, probably Dr. Parr first filled the young man's head with the liberty-loving thoughts destined to play such an important part in Merry's turbulent future.[43] With Parr's liberal notions stamped forever upon

---

[40] London *Times*, December 20, 1790; William B. Wood, *Personal Recollections of the Stage* (Philadelphia, 1855), 63.
[41] The main source for Merry's background and early life is David Erskine Baker, *Biographia Dramatica* (London, 1812), 507.
[42] *The Thespian Dictionary*, p. ME.
[43] See M. Ray Adams, "Samuel Parr, 'The whig Johnson,'" in Adams, *Studies in the Literary Background of English Radicalism* (Lancaster, 1947), 267–311.

him, Merry entered Christ's College, Cambridge; but his attendance was irregular and he soon dropped out. After briefly considering a law career while attending Lincoln's Inn (one of the
Inns of Court), Merry abandoned academic pursuits for the
fashionable life of London. Wealthy, handsome, and charming,
he cut a dashing figure in social circles, especially as an officer in
the Horse Guards, in which he had purchased a commission with
the inheritance received upon the death of his father. Enjoying
an extremely gay life during his military career, he admitted in
later years to spending £17,000 in a span of three years, a prof-
ligacy which ultimately forced him, at the age of twenty-five, to
sell his commission and follow a nomadic existence on the Continent.[44] By 1784 he had arrived in Florence, where he quickly
became part of English and Italian literary circles.

During the years spent in Florence, Merry's name first became
identified with the term "Della Crusca." In July, 1783, prior to
Merry's arrival in Italy, the Austrian ruler of Florence, Grand
Duke Leopold of Tuscany, had suppressed the famous *Accademia
della Crusca*.[45] Leopold created in its place the *Real Accademia
Fiorentina* in an attempt to keep a controlling hand on academi-
cians who threatened his power with their political poetry. Merry
accepted membership in the newly formed academy, apparently
as a means of aiding former Della Cruscans, who continued to
resist the oppressive Austrian ruler. And the duke may have been
eager for the Englishman to join the society so that he could keep
an eye on Merry, his rival for the attention of the Countess Cow-
per, the duke's mistress. As a member of the *Accademia Fiorentina*, the liberal Merry rebelled against Leopold's censorship of
literary composition. At the same time, Merry's defiant spirit encouraged his aspirations as a poet, for it appears that it was Merry
who inspired his own English coterie and several Italian poets to
compose verses imitating Italian rhymes and meters as an attempt
to uphold the venerated ideals of the abolished *Accademia della*

[44] Wood, *Personal Recollections*, 63.
[45] The chief source for the Italian political background is Roderick R. Marshall, *Italy in English Literature, 1755–1815* (New York, 1934), 175–77.

Crusca. The collected efforts of the group were published as *Florence Miscellany* in 1785. The verses and their authors soon attracted attention in England, where several of the poems appeared in such periodicals as *European Magazine, London Chronicle,* and *Gentleman's Magazine.*[46]

In the summer of 1787, while Merry was still on the Continent, his poems attracted further notice when they appeared in the *World,* an "upper-class social journal" established by Edward Topham, Merry's old Cambridge friend and fellow officer in the Horse Guards.[47] Instead of using his own name, however, Merry signed the poetry "Della Crusca." Apparently the nom de plume served as testimony to his admiration for the former members of the academy, for their resistance to oppression, and for their promotion of artistic standards, ideals dear to Merry's liberal spirit and literary inclinations. Although Merry wrote on a variety of subjects under the signature "Della Crusca," one of his romantic poems, "Adieu and Recall to Love," published June 29, 1787, attracted the attention of Mrs. Hannah Cowley. Her poetical response, signed "Anna Matilda," initiated a two-year sentimental exchange of verse in the pages of the *World.* The correspondence not only captured the imagination of the reading public but it inspired a rash of similar poetical correspondence by persons who signed themselves by such titles as Arley, the Bard, Cesario, and Emma.[48] Collectively the writers became acclaimed as Della Cruscans. Public enthusiasm for the sentimental verses reached such momentum that selected works collected into *The British Album* enjoyed no less than four London editions between 1789 and 1792, and a Boston edition in 1793. The Merry-Cowley exchange came to an end in 1789 when the newspaper lovers met for the first time and discovered that the lady was forty-six and the gentleman thirty-four.[49] If the meeting was disappointing to Merry, surely his newly acquired fame as Della Crusca was not.

[46] James L. Clifford, "Robert Merry—a pre-Byronic Hero," *Bulletin of the John Rylands Library,* XXVII (1942), 74.
[47] Ibid.
[48] See *The British Album* (Boston, 1793).
[49] Clifford, "Robert Merry," 92.

The personal character of Anne's future husband emerges from his correspondence and from descriptions by those who knew him. After examining Merry's correspondence with Mrs. Hester Lynch Piozzi, her biographer James L. Clifford concluded that the correspondence

> shows the erratic idiosyncrasies of a gifted man who somehow lacked the balance and discipline needed in a great writer. Merry had all the surface traits of a Lord Byron—the spectacular love affairs, the masochistic sense of evil of his own nature, the feeling of tremendous inner power and pride in his own resources. And he had, too, many of Byron's redeeming traits—his hatred of oppression, his intense feeling about human freedom, his passionate worship of beauty. But something was missing, and instead of the misunderstood genius he thought himself to be, Merry appears to us, after a century and a half, merely a foolish *poseur*, vainly striving to impress the world with his greatness.[50]

No doubt this evaluation was also influenced by Mrs. Piozzi's many references to Merry in her diary, one of which is particularly unflattering: "Merry is a dissipated Man become truly wicked: by Accident rather than by Principle however: of elegant and airy Manners, but of a Melancholy and apparently Conscience-smitten Spirit. His Distresses interest one's Tenderness, his Courage & Learning claim one's true Respect; Merry is a Scholar, a Soldier, a Wit and a Whig, beautiful in his Person, gay in his Conversation, scornful of a feeble Soul, but full of Reverence for a good one though it be not great. Were Merry *daringly*, instead of artfully wicked, he would resemble Pierre."[51]

Mrs. Piozzi's comments, written when the Merry-Piozzi family friendship was on the wane, are a distinct contrast to the phrases of warm regard used by John Bernard, Merry's fellow member of London's convivial Beefsteak Club and close associate in America. Bernard spoke of Merry as his "dearly esteemed friend" and described him as he appeared at meetings in the late 1780's.

---

[50] *Ibid.*, 74.
[51] *Ibid.*, 86. Pierre is a character in Thomas Otway's *Venice Preserv'd*.

Of all men in the Club, Merry had the greatest proportion of that which, in my "Scale," I intended by the term good-humour,—that cheerful, placid, and benevolent mould of mind which can bear all its own peculiarities being laughed at, without wishing to laugh at another's in return. Never was a man's name a greater echo to his character than Merry's. . . . Merry seemed to live in a perpetual spring; all was sunshine and freshness with him, and his heart overflowed with its happiness, like a sparkling fountain. He was not so witty as Andrews, or so original; but he was rather the pleasanter companion of the two, for he had more oil and less vinegar. . . . Merry couldn't write satire, (it was as little in his head as his heart).[52]

Such descriptions typify the extreme responses Merry elicited from those who knew him. Nevertheless, from all accounts, his intelligence, wit, and charm made him welcome in the club or drawing room.

Unfortunately, these social assets could not make a dramatist of him. As well as receiving attacks because of its political nature, *The Picture of Paris*, his first dramatic attempt, was condemned as unstageworthy. The *Times* expressed regret that so much money and energy had been expended on the pantomime and suggested that "at all events, we must earnestly recommend, amidst other curtailments, the total absence of *Holman* and Miss *Brunton*, whose dramatic talents ought not to be degraded by the trash of the pantomime,—the serious scene was well written— but it wants interest, and therefore wants everything."[53] Apparently Anne agreed with the suggestion of withdrawal, for she (along with other members of the company), disgusted with the "fooleries" in several scenes, refused to continue in the pantomime.[54] Harris may have fined her, as he did several performers, for such a breach of articles, with the end result of damaged relations between actress and manager. Amazingly enough, even with the disapproval of critics and actors, the pantomime was

[52] Bernard, *Retrospections of the Stage*, II, 93.
[53] London *Times* December 21, 1790.
[54] James Fennell, *An Apology for the Life of James Fennell* (Philadelphia, 1814), 306.

advertised thirty-five times during the rest of the season. Perhaps the topical, controversial nature of the pantomime drew play-goers, or possibly Harris was forced to offer the after-piece because he had invested large sums of money in it at a time when the Covent Garden box office was suffering. Coincidental with the discouraging box office was the announcement that Anne Brunton and John Quick were abandoning Covent Garden boards at the end of the season. Consequently, the *Times* rebuked the theatre for "a loss which that stage in its present poverty of actors could ill afford." Almost as if to emphasize the significance of such a loss, only a day earlier the same newspaper had testified: "Till the recovery of Mrs. Siddons—MELPOMENE, if she acts wisely—will watch by the bed of her best friend—and never venture out—except to leave a card of compliment with MISS BRUN-TON." But by the end of February Anne resolved her differences with the management, and the *Times* happily announced that she was still "to continue the sweetest and fairest dramatic flower of COVENT GARDEN."[55]

Noteworthy among the new roles she created that spring is Zoriana in Robert Merry's second dramatic attempt, *Lorenzo*. The tragedy probably provided the couple the opportunity to deepen their relationship, but it did not further Merry's career as a dramatist nor Anne's as an actress. The role of Zoriana demanded a portrayal of a violent, rejected wife who poisons herself in despair but survives long enough to stab her husband's assailant. As one critic suggested, the casting might have been better had she and Mrs. Pope exchanged roles, that is, if Anne had played Seraphina, Lorenzo's gentle truelove. The acting was generally approved, however: the tragedy "was extremely well acted throughout, and the performers much more correct than is usual on a first presentation." The play itself, "more calculated for the closet than the stage," seemed to borrow incidents too obviously from *Isabella*, *Zara*, and *Romeo and Juliet*, and "the construction of the plot sufficiently proves him [Merry] to have ventured much beyond his dramatic depth." The only favorable remarks

[55] London *Times*, January 22, 21, February 28, 1791.

referred to the play's language, which was described as "elegant and poetical" and bearing "evident marks of coming from the pen of a person possessed of a fervid imagination."[56] But with its many weaknesses the play could not sustain more than six performances.

Anne learned two more roles that spring, bringing the total number of new parts to six for the 1790–1791 season. Altogether she enacted seventeen characterizations in fifty-three performances, twenty less than the year before and ten less than the season of 1788–1789. Nevertheless disappointments in her career may have been offset by broader considerations of her entire future. By the middle of June the actress had given a promise of marriage to Robert Merry.[57] To Boaden it was not unforeseen: "To have yielded to the ardour and accomplishments of Merry could be a matter of no surprise to any person who had enjoyed his society. Bating his tendency to play, which was a fever in him that nothing could render intermittent, he was one of the most original and captivating men whom I have ever known."[58] A poem written by Merry during their courtship and dated June 30, 1791, is evidence of an ardor which may have helped to captivate Anne.

TO

A——E. B——N.

Think not, TRANSCENDENT MAID! my woe
    Shall ever trouble thy repose;
The mind no lasting pang can know,
    Which lets the tongue that pang disclose.

Sorrow is *sacred* when 'tis *true*,
    In deep concealment proudly dwells,
And seems its passion to subdue,
    When most th' impulsive throb compels.

---

[56] *European Magazine*, XIX (April, 1791), 308; London *Times*, April 6, 1791; *European Magazine*, XIX (April, 1791), 308.
[57] London *Times*, June 18, 1791.
[58] Boaden, *Memoirs of John Philip Kemble*, II, 46.

For HE who dares *assert* his grief,
    Who boasts the anguish he may prove,
Obtains, perhaps, the wish'd relief,
    BUT O! THE TRAITOR DOES NOT LOVE.
The LOVER is a *Man afraid*,
    Has neither grace, nor ease, nor art,
Embarass'd, comfortless dimay'd
    He sinks the VICTIM OF HIS HEART.

He feels his own demerits most,
    When he should most *aspire* to gain,
And is at length completely *lost*,
    Because he cannot *urge* his pain.

But tho' he be so much subdu'd,
    And ev'ry scene of spirit leave,
As if he mourn'd for all he view'd,
    As if he only *liv'd to grieve.*

Yet let his FAIR-ONE'S wrongs be told,
    Sudden he rushes forth to save,
The Forest's King is not so bold!
    O! IF HE LOVES HE MUST BE BRAVE.

And if, alas! her hand should bless
    Some more attractive youth than HE;
He never would adore the less,
    But glory in his agony.

He'd see her to the altar led,
    And still command his struggling sigh,
Nor would he let one tear be shed,
    He'd triumph then;—FOR THEN HE'D DIE.
                 DELLA CRUSCA.[59]

59 *The British Album,* 323–24.

The verses suggest that Merry may still have had a rival as late as June 30, only a week before the published date of their wedding, July 7. The losing rival may have been Frederick Reynolds, who did not assist at the "nuptial solemnities," because "with a heart rather sad" he "set off yesterday on an excursion to the Isle of Wight." The ceremony did not take place on July 7, however, and the *Times* subsequently suggested that "Melpomene would do wisely to forbid the Banns between *Merry* and Miss Brunton; —we know not what will become [of] the tragic Dame when deprived of the kind of offices of her FAVOURITE child!"[60] Finally the wedding took place on August 27, 1791, at St. Martin's church, and the bride returned to Covent Garden two weeks later, opening the season with *The Dramatist*, September 12, 1791.[61] On that occasion "Mrs. *Merry* had very little to do as Miss Courtney, but to receive the warm congratulations of the audience on her late marriage, and surely never bride saw company with merrier faces." A few days later the same newspaper approved her acting "wifely in retaining her real name in the bills," a practice the actress continued throughout her career and her three marriages.[62]

Mrs. Merry played her usual repertoire that fall, sharing the boards again with Mrs. Esten, who had received a Covent Garden engagement after considerable pressure in her behalf had been exerted on Harris by influential friends.[63] Performing roles which Mrs. Merry had been known to portray, the newcomer probably served at least as a partial threat to Anne throughout the year. Nevertheless Anne earned praise for her standard characterizations as well as her new roles. Her enactment of Cordelia in November "was as great a treat as Holman's EDGAR." In the December performance of James Thomson's tragedy of *Tancred and Sigismunda* she "gained much approbation."[64] Understandably critics did not ignore Mrs. Merry's off-nights. As Adelaide in *The Count of Narbonne*, she "was not entirely earnest," and her

[60] London *Times*, July 6, 7, 9, 1791.
[61] *Ibid.*, September 1, 1791.
[62] *Ibid.*, September 13, 15, 1791.
[63] Haslewood, *The Secret History of the Green-Room*, II, 133–34.
[64] London *Times*, November 5, December 22, 1791.

Lady Amaranth (a replacement for Mrs. Pope who was ill) in O'Keeffe's *Wild Oats*, was "not at all moved with the spirit of the Author!"[65]

While Mrs. Merry met the weekly triumphs and failures of theatre life, her husband pursued his literary and political interests which eventually proved disastrous to the young couple. Merry "became perfectly *rabid* with the French revolution; associated himself with the radical press, and . . . by degrees he detached himself from men who could not echo, and disdained to humour him; and though complexionally indolent, his political passion lashed him into a daily ridicule of all that ages have respected. . . . Over this transformation even the muse possessed no power, and the poet and the gentleman vanished together."[66]

However, in the first year of their marriage, the literary muse was probably the chief source of distress for the Merrys. The year 1791 marked the year of publication of William Gifford's successful satirical attack on Della Cruscan poetry *The Baviad*, which turned the tide of public enthusiasm against the sentimental versifiers and toppled Merry from his celebrated literary perch.[67] In spite of ridicule and criticism, as a means to fame Merry attempted a new medium, opera. He and a composer, Joseph Mazzinghi, collaborated in a production entitled *Magician no Conjuror* which opened at Covent Garden, February 2, 1792. Unhappily, it met with even less success than *Lorenzo*, playing only four performances. Almost as if to accentuate Merry's failure, Thomas Holcroft's new comedy *The Road to Ruin*, with Mrs. Merry playing a leading role, opened the same month and commanded thirty-eight performances for the playhouse

---

[65] *Ibid.*, September 20, December 22, 1791.

[66] Boaden, *Memoirs of John Philip Kemble*, II, 47.

[67] For an evaluation of Gifford's criticism see Roy Benjamin Clark, *William Gifford: Tory Satirist, Critic, and Editor* (New York, 1930), 35–80. In addition, see Clifford as cited above and Edward Bostetter, "The Original Della Cruscans and the Florence Miscellany," *Huntington Library Quarterly*, XIX (May, 1956) 277–300. Clifford believes Gifford correctly identified the chief weakness of the Della Cruscan poets "in their excessive use of artificial ornament, their needless obscurity, their orgies of sentiment." Bostetter points out that the attack was out of proportion to the significance of the poetry and that it was probably partly politically inspired.

and £900 for the playwright.[68] Considering these embarrassments, it must have been a relief, in spite of Mrs. Merry's relatively successful season of fourteen roles and sixty performances, for the couple to withdraw from the public eye at the end of the season, when Mrs. Merry terminated her Covent Garden engagement as well as her British acting career. Family pressure also must have entered into the decision, for Merry's relatives disapproved of the marriage and the actress' career. Merry's sister revealed family concern for the marriage over a cup of tea with Fanny Burney, who noted the conversation in her diary in November, 1791: "Miss Merry, too, was of the party; she is sister of Liberty Mr. Merry. . . . The sister and her aunt, with whom she lives, were much hurt by his alliance; and especially by his continuing his wife on the stage, and with their own name. She remonstrated against this indelicacy; but he answered she ought to be proud he had brought a woman of such virtue and talents into the family."[69] That Merry's politics might also be distressing to his family became evident in the rest of the conversation, for Merry's sister made it quite clear that her own politics were the reverse of her brother's.

Although it may have been convenient for the Merrys to bow to family wishes with Mrs. Merry's retirement from the stage, Robert Merry did not change his politics. Shortly after Covent Garden doors closed for the season on June 1, the *Times* announced that "Mrs. MERRY, the Actress, and her husband, are gone to France."[70] There, without any feeling of restraint, Merry entered into the political activities of the hour. If he enjoyed observing the principles of democracy at work, Merry was also forced to watch the French Revolution move into the hands of the extremists. The Merrys arrived in France in time to witness the beginning of the violent and bloody second stage of the revolution initiated on August 10, 1792, with the storming of the royal palace, followed by the September massacres, the trial and be-

[68] Thomas Holcroft, *Memoirs of Thomas Holcroft Written by himself and Continued by William Hazlitt* (London, 1816), 161.
[69] Charlotte Barrett (ed.), *Diary and Letters of Madam D'Arblay, July, 1791–April, 1802* (London, 1904–1905), 39–40.
[70] London *Times*, June 6, 1792.

heading of Louis XVI, and the Reign of Terror (1793–94). Merry balked, however, at attending the trial of Louis XVI, for as passionately as the poet supported the principles of the French Revolution, there is no evidence that he endorsed its violence.[71]

Before the September massacres, when the new French Republic was in danger of falling to European forces, Merry expressed interest in going to America. James Fennell, a former Covent Garden stage mate of Mrs. Merry, who was spending his honeymoon in Paris, recorded in his memoirs not only Merry's proposal to emigrate to the United States, but also his willingness for his wife to return to the stage. Moreover Merry proposed that the two couples sail for America where his wife and Fennell "conjointly can command your situations on the theatre."[72] Fennell declined the idea at the time but later changed his mind and sailed for America the following year. When France declared war on England, February 1, 1793, the Merrys remained in Paris until summer, returning to London after Merry's friend the famed French artist Jacques Louis David secured a passport for them.[73]

Upon their return to England, their life was by no means a settled one. Merry's acknowledged sympathies with France made him distrusted by the British government. In September the Merrys and radical Charles Pigott sought the free air of Geneva but abandoned plans at Harwich upon learning of the dangerous travel conditions in Holland and on the Rhine.[74] The couple next located in Scarborough, where at off-season prices they enjoyed a comfortable house overlooking the sea. From Scarborough, Merry wrote to his friend the poet Samuel Rogers, reporting work on a novel and distress that his mail was being read by post-office spies. In December he sent Rogers his adaptation of a French play, *Fenelon* by Marie Joseph Chenier, hoping that Harris at Covent Garden would accept it without knowing the translator's

[71] *Monthly Magazine and British Register*, VII (April, 1799), 257.
[72] Fennell, *An Apology for . . . James Fennell*, 325.
[73] *Monthly Magazine and British Register*, 257.
[74] P. W. Clayden, *The Early Life of Samuel Rogers* (London, 1887), 247.

name. By the following June the Merrys had moved to Brecon Ash, near Norwich, where they entertained William Godwin.[75] No doubt the two liberals discussed the arrest of their non-conformist friend Horne Tooke for high treason, on the grounds of advocating free government. Such oppressive actions by the Pitt government probably intensified Merry's interest in emi-grating to the more democratic United States. In October, 1794, he again expressed such thoughts in a letter to Rogers, asking his advice on how to proceed.[76] In the same letter he spoke of his financial difficulty, and it was, no doubt, financial distress which persuaded the couple that Mrs. Merry should resume her acting career in England. For this reason Merry sought the help of an old friend, John Taylor, an ultra-Tory and editor of the *Morning Post*. Merry asked Taylor to persuade Harris to renew his wife's engagement at Covent Garden, but the manager declined on the grounds that "he should be subject to attacks from her hus-band in the newspapers, unless she was allowed to perform every character she liked, and to be provided with the most expensive dresses."[77]

After Harris' refusal, Merry asked Taylor to make a comparable request of Stephen Kemble, manager of the theatre at Newcastle-upon-Tyne. This negotiation was never completed because of what appears to have been an injudicious newspaper attack on Taylor by Merry in November, 1795. Although Merry later apolo-gized, the breach between the two never healed and Stephen Kemble did not hire Anne.

The exact decline of the Merry's fortunes in the next year is not known, but that their financial position was desperate be-comes clear from Godwin's report that while visiting the Merrys in Norwich in the summer of 1796, he paid a £200-debt to pre-vent Robert from being thrown into jail.[78] Soon after, when Thomas Wignell offered Anne an engagement at the Chestnut

[75] Charles Kegan Paul, *William Godwin, His Friends and Contemporaries* (Boston, 1876), 118.
[76] Clayden, *The Early Life of Samuel Rogers*, 249.
[77] John Taylor, *Records of My Life* (London, 1832) II, 271–72.
[78] Paul, *William Godwin*, 154.

Street theatre in Philadelphia, one can well imagine that the proposal was enthusiastically accepted. One by one the avenues of both political and financial independence had closed to the couple. Any chance of Merry's recapturing his prestige as a poet had been prevented by William Gifford's successful ridicule. Merry's plays had never received encouragement by critics or the public and could not, therefore, be a source of fame or gain. Moreover his political sympathies kept him continually under the suspicious eye of the government. On the Continent the revolutionary turmoil made existence equally undesirable, if not impossible. And although the Merrys were willing to solve their financial difficulties by ignoring family sensibilities and returning Mrs. Merry to the British stage, her husband's political activities made this impossible.

When the Merrys boarded the *Sansom*, bound for America on September 19, 1796, Mrs. Merry may have been reminded of a similar adventure eleven years before when she left Bath for the London stage. No longer the fledgling actress, she was an experienced performer, equipped to meet the demands of leading roles at the leading American playhouse. She was fortified by seven years' exposure to successes and failures at Covent Garden and by the technique and experience of 50 roles in more than 352 performances. Undoubtedly, too, she was more knowledgeable in the emotional range of life, a knowledge acquired through the stress of a marriage marked by financial and political anxiety. The New World offered her marriage financial relief and stability, but it also offered her career the opportunity to test and perhaps fulfill her dramatic talent. Significantly the Merrys shared the voyage with Thomas Wignell and William Warren, both of whom subsequently became husbands to Anne Brunton Merry. Immediately before her, however, was the long voyage and a new career in a new land.

III

The First Season in America

1796-1797

On October 18, 1796, one month after the Merrys boarded the *Sansom*, an American pilot steered the vessel up the East River into the New York harbor,[1] and within the next week the travelers had completed their journey to Philadelphia. The Merrys remained in Philadelphia, unlike Wignell and several of the other actors who joined the rest of the Chestnut Street company then performing in Baltimore. With more than a month before Mrs. Merry's first appearance, the couple had a comfortable amount of time during which to rest from their ocean voyage and orient themselves to their new home. The largest city in the Union and the seat of the state and federal governments, it possessed one of the most cosmopolitan societies in the United States. In addition to testing the efficiency of the Constitution as an instrument of government, the citizens had the advantage of a library containing 15,000 volumes, a university with 510 students, a literary society with some 450 members, a museum devoted to the natural history of science and art, and thirty-three churches representing thirteen different faiths.[2] Not the least of the city's claims was the handsomest theatre in the United States, opened in 1794 by Wignell and his musician-partner Alexander Reinagle, with a company of fifty-six actors and musicians.[3] Located on the

---

[1] William I. Warren, Journals (Channing Pollock Theatre Collection, Howard University, Washington, D. C.), October 18, 1796, hereinafter cited as Warren, Journals.

[2] Moreau de Saint-Méry, *American Journey*, *1793–1797*, trans. and ed. by Kenneth Roberts and Anna M. Roberts (New York, 1947), 346.

[3] Thomas Clark Pollock, *The Philadelphia Theatre in the Eighteenth Century* (Philadelphia, 1933), 54–55.

north side of Chestnut Street above Sixth, the playhouse was a
short half block diagonally across the street from Congress Hall,
the seat of the national legislature. A typically Georgian playhouse of the late eighteenth century, its stage, thirty-six feet
wide and seventy-one feet deep, extended into a raked auditorium containing thirteen rows of benches where women as well
as men sat surrounded by three tiers of boxes accommodating the
fashionable patrons. As many as twelve hundred spectators could
enjoy an evening's performance, and in 1805 enlargement of the
playhouse increased its capacity to two thousand playgoers.[4] The
actors performed before controllable oil lamps while the audience,
illuminated by four-branched chandeliers attached to the boxes,
watched from an auditorium elegantly decorated with gilded
scrolls and carvings. "When Gen'l Washington visited the theatre, the east stage box was decorated with the United States coat
of arms. . . . Mr. Wignell, dress'd in black and powdered, with
two silver candlesticks, would wait at the box door to receive him
and light him to his seat. A guard of soldiers where [sic] in attendance on the occasion, one soldier at each stage door, four
placet [sic] in the gallery, with the assistance of our high con-
stable."[5]

Appropriately Anne made her American debut in a tragedy in
which she had opened several Covent Garden seasons, *Romeo
and Juliet.* Her Romeo was John Pollard Moreton, often called
the American Holman, who had been a favorite with American
audiences since 1794. Four others who had crossed the ocean with
her also participated in the opening production of 1796. L'Estrange portrayed Capulet, Wignell enacted Mercutio, Warren
played Friar Laurence, and Mrs. L'Estrange was the Nurse. Billed
as "late the principal actress at Covent-Garden," Mrs. Merry attracted the greatest share of attention from a "numerous and
attentive audience" offering her "loud and repeated plaudits."

4 James Mease, *The Picture of Philadelphia* (Philadelphia, 1811), 331; de Saint-
Méry, *American Journey*, 346; Mease, *The Picture of Philadelphia*, 330–31.
5 John Durang, *The Memoir of John Durang: American Actor, 1785–1816,* ed.
Alan S. Downer (Pittsburgh, 1966), 105.

Two separate reviews in Philadelphia's *Gazette of the United States* supplied details of the performance. "Dramaticus" praised her for those qualities admired in the British Isles: "her form interesting and graceful; and her countenance, tho' marked by feminine sweetness, has yet the power to mark the passions with all the energy of truth. Her voice is the most melodious we ever heard; and her action natural, easy and appropriate." Additional comments indicate that Anne's portrayal of Juliet was stronger than it had been in London: "In her speech, act IV, when she drinks the sleeping draught, she thrill'd every heart with horrid sympathy; and her dying scene was inimitably fine. In justice we must say, that this elegant and powerful actress is a most valuable acquisition to the American stage." The reviewer also admired the "new, rich and elegant" costumes, especially because "they were not modern . . . but they were suited to the age and country where the scene is laid." In the same newspaper another critic signed "W" provided further insight into Mrs. Merry's performance by comparing her to Mrs. Marshall and Mrs. Whitlock (Mrs. Siddons' sister), both of whom had previously performed the role in Philadelphia. Apparently Mrs. Merry exerted force and energy which Mrs. Marshall lacked, but not the "masculine coarseness" which was Mrs. Whitlock's failing. A decided artistic triumph, Anne could not "fail at once to establish her own fame, and to reflect honour on the American drama."[6] Moreover the debut brought twelve hundred dollars into the company treasury and her portrait into many homes.[7] On the day following her debut *Claypoole's American Daily Advertiser* announced the availability of Mrs. Merry's portrait as Juliet: plain, fifty cents, and colored, one dollar. The opening week of the theatre season also introduced three other shipmates of Mrs. Merry. James Byrne and his wife, engaged to perform and produce pantomimes and ballets, made their first appearance on Wednesday; and on Friday, Thomas Abthorpe Cooper, a young tragic actor of great

[6] Philadelphia, *Gazette of the United States and Philadelphia Daily Advertiser*, December 7, 1796, hereinafter cited as *Gazette of the United States*.
[7] Warren, Journals, December 5, 1796.

promise but no extensive experience, gave a debut performance as Macbeth.

Because the theatre normally gave presentations on only three nights a week, Mrs. Merry next offered her "splendid talents" on the following Monday when, as Calista (*The Fair Penitent*), she "exceeded expectation" and "furnished a standard of excellence in acting that will long be resorted to." If unconvinced before, "the best judges" now conceded that her acting had "never been equalled in America."[8] Moreton, portraying "gallant, gay Lothario," and Cooper, enacting the faithful friend Horatio, received praise; but Mrs. Merry eclipsed all others. "It would be difficult to give an accurate idea of the superior merit of Mrs. Merry in Calista. A more chaste and finished piece of acting could not be seen. She touched every feeling of the heart—Every sentence had effect. If nature is the standard by which we are to judge of acting, she certainly is the first performer we ever saw—the countenance, the action, the tone of voice, all corresponding to produce the most charming effect." In another critique Anne again withstood further comparison with Mrs. Whitlock, even though in the first part of the play the reviewer preferred Mrs. Whitlock's performance of Calista. "In many instances, Mrs. Merry's accent and cadence were false, and the emphasis improperly laid; and words emphasized that did not require to be." However, in the final act, "she crowned her former fame, and effaced from the mind, all conceptions of the possibility of her being surpassed. In the parting scene with her father, she wrung every heart with feeling for her ideal anguish, and forced the tear of sympathy from every eye." Another journal exclaimed, "What pleasure must not the lover of drama anticipate from the capacity manifested by Mrs. Merry and Mr. Cooper on Monday evening."[9]

After only two performances a critic, "Philo-Theatricus," provided an index to Anne's success by evaluating the new actors in

---

[8] Philadelphia, *Gazette of the United States*, December 14, 1796; Philadelphia, *Gazette and Universal Daily Advertizer*, December 13, 1796, hereinafter cited as Philadelphia *Gazette*.

[9] Philadelphia, *Gazette of the United States*, December 13, 14, 1796; Philadelphia, *Aurora General Advertiser*, December 15, 1796.

the company with the old. Graded "more from public, than private opinion," the players earned the following scores:

Performers Absent		New Performers	
Mrs. Whitlock	13	Mrs. Merry	15
Shaw	10	Mechtler	4
Marshall	9	Miss L'Estrange	4
Cleveland	5	Mrs. L'Estrange	3
Green	4	Mr. Cooper	11
Rowson	3	Warren	9
Miss Broadhurst	10	Fox	6
Mr. Fennell	13	L'Estrange	4
Bates	12		—
Chalmers	12		56
Whitlock	11		
Marshall	7		
Cleveland	5		
Green	5		

119

Mrs. Merry, "that elegant actress, this paragon, this excellent theatrical star," not only earned more points than Mrs. Marshall and Mrs. Whitlock, but she was the only performer awarded a perfect score of 15.[10]

In her third appearance before Philadelphia audiences, the newcomer demonstrated her versatility by performing in the sentimental comedy *The Child of Nature*. She again enacted the role of Amanthis which she had originated and become so well identified with in England. American audiences were also "fascinated" by her "faithful portrait of arch simplicity, tender emotion and filial affection." Further approval from "Dramaticus" commended the honesty and control which became hallmarks of her performances: "She never o'er-steps the modesty of nature, she seeks not by artifice to entrap applause, but while she satisfies the understanding her appeal is to the heart."[11]

[10] Philadelphia, *Gazette of the United States*, December 16, 1796.
[11] *Ibid.*, December 19, 1796.

As the approval mounted, Anne's work increased. In her first month at the Chestnut Street theatre she gave nine performances of five different roles, including the first new role she learned in America, Emily Tempest, in Richard Cumberland's *The Wheel of Fortune*. But December was only an indication of the interesting and busy months ahead. Anne performed for the first time before President Washington in early January when "by desire" the theatre presented *The Child of Nature*. For some unknown reason she performed the Marchioness Merida on that occasion instead of Amanthis.[12] In the last part of the same month, she had a brief vacation from regular performing chores when the theatre closed for a week while "the masterly pencil of Melbourne . . . engaged in producing the most grand and picturesque scenery ever exhibited on this, and perhaps any Theatre" for the "celebrated spectacle" of *Columbus* by Thomas Morton. The elaborate preparations not only included new scenery, but new machinery, decorations, costumes by Gibbons, and music composed by Reinagle.[13] The managers also promised spectacular processions and pageants designed by Byrne, including the first landing of Columbus, a storm and earthquake with a "grand eruption from a volcano," and a march of sacrifice and procession to the execution of the Indian maid Cora, played by Mrs. Merry. The advance publicity so successfully excited the public curiosity that on the night of the first performance the theatre "passages were not free from a croud till half an hour after the curtain rose," while many playgoers were turned away.[14] Appropriately, manager Wignell spoke the prologue, half of which was specially written for the occasion by Robert Merry.[15] As the title suggests, the historical drama concerns Columbus and the mutinous behavior of some of his crew after arriving in the New World. Much of the spectacle's interest, however, centers on the romance of the Spaniard Alonzo and Cora, an Indian priestess. Because of her sacred vows

[12] Pollock, *The Philadelphia Theatre*, 319.
[13] Philadelphia, *Gazette of the United States*, January 28, February 4, 1797.
[14] Philadelphia, *Aurora General Advertiser*, February 2, 1797.
[15] *Ibid.*, February 4, 1797.

Cora cannot return Alonzo's love under pain of her own death or that of her family. During an earthquake and volcanic eruption Alonzo rescues her from the temple and the couple flee together. After the storm and volcano subside, duty parts the young lovers and Cora returns to the temple. Although the discovery of her temporary absence dooms her, Alonzo persuades the chief to spare her. But a defiant priest ignores the reprieve and Alonzo is forced to rescue Cora again, just as she is about to be killed. Once more their happiness is threatened by the treasonous Spanish troops, but the sudden victorious arrival of Columbus saves the lovers and concludes the play on a happy note. These startling reversals in the action and the elaborate effects captivated the Philadelphia audience. A vivid account of the more spectacular scenes appeared in the newspaper the following day:

> The brilliancy of the spectacle and decorations produced universal pleasure; till the representation of the earthquake and the eruption from a volcano really inspired those feelings which a real representation could only increase. The horrid subterraneous sounds, the rocking trees, the violent destruction of houses, the sight of falling ruins, presented perhaps, as true a delineation of such an awful scene as description can afford.—Persons, who have often witnessed exhibitions of this kind in Europe, declare the volcano not to be surpassed by any representation they ever saw.[16]

Acknowledging the performers' contribution, the newspaper indicates that the acting was not wholly subordinate to the exciting effects. As the "feeling, gallant" Alonzo, Moreton played with great sensitivity," while as Cora, Mrs. Merry received "deep attention . . . [which] must have been more flattering to her than the loudest plaudits that could have been bestowed . . . while she was playing Cora we forgot we were in a theatre; we forgot the accomplished actress, and beheld only the charming Indian maid that was to be devoted to the sacrifice."[17] Moreover the reviewer attributed Moreton's general excellence for the season to the

---

[16] *Ibid.*, February 1, 1797.
[17] Philadelphia, *Gazette of the United States*, February 3, 1797.

inspiration of her "exquisite acting." The only negative criticism concerned the costumes, which seem to have distressed late eighteenth century taste for the "natural." Anne's costume, especially, violated historical appropriateness, for had she "left out the golden star that adorn'd her bosom, she might have acted Sophia in the 'Road to Ruin.' " Incongruous costumes could not lessen the sensational appeal of what (with its thirteen performances) became unquestionably the greatest success of the entire year.

In spite of Anne's acclaim, the Chestnut Street theatre was not always overflowing when she performed. Her first appearance as Belvidera (*Venice Preserv'd*) in January drew a sparse house. But the size of the audience could not diminish the quality of her performance; her Belvidera satisfied spectators who shed tears as "unequivocal proof of the intrinsic merit of this admirable drama, and of the justice done it by the performers."[18]

Throughout the spring Mrs. Merry increased her renown in performances of well-established roles, as well as new ones. In Thomas Morton's *The Way to Get Married* she portrayed one of her most popular new characterizations, Julia Faulkner, the essence of "filial affection and feminine diffidence."[19]

Although extravagantly praised, Anne did not escape criticism. As noted in her first performance of Juliet, her accents and cadence as well as her emphasis were sometimes misplaced; this would result in incorrect readings. In her first American performance of Euphrasia in March, a pattern of "emphasizing excessively" was distractingly apparent. Still this weakness could not obscure her "brilliant" acting or her "better claim to perfection than any actress we know of."[20] The same evening's program offered a two-act farce, *The Enchanted Flute* ("written in America," and "never performed before,"), which Warren attributes to Merry. The farce earned two performances and favorable ac-

[18] *Ibid.*, February 6, 1797.
[19] Thomas Morton, *The Way to Get Married, The British Drama*, XII (London, n.d.), 82.
[20] Philadelphia, *Gazette of the United States*, March 4, 1797.

knowledgement by a local critic who assigned the work "in the scale of merit, far, very far, above the generality of Farces."[21] Such approval may have encouraged the management, within the same month, to invest company energy and expense in a production of Merry's full-length tragedy *The Abbey of St. Augustine.* Elaborate preparations for the production closed the theatre for one performance while Milbourne mounted new scenery and decorations.[22] The play drew respectable box-office receipts of $760 and was "well received altho [sic]—the heroes being Monks—and the Heroine a Nun . . . very much diminished the interest of the scenes." The tragedy apparently held attention for two more evenings and in spite of "a stir . . . made to support the tragedy" for additional performances, Warren accurately predicted that in the future it would "rest in peace and quietness."[23]

On March 29 Anne enjoyed the first benefit performance of the season. She used the occasion to advance her husband's playwriting career by performing in his *Lorenzo*, retitled *The Ransomed Slave.* In the American production, instead of Zoriana, she portrayed the sentimental heroine Zeraphine, which Mrs. Pope had performed in London. The benefit receipts of $1,025 probably attest to the public's admiration for Mrs. Merry's acting rather than her husband's playwriting, for there is no record of a second performance of the work.

A listing of the Philadelphia benefit of 1797 receipts reveals that Mrs. Merry outdistanced most of the company in popularity and indicates her value to the Chestnut Street theatre organization:

Mrs. Merry	$1025	Harwood	1206
Moreton	865	Warrell	516
Cooper	834	Bates	869
Mrs. Oldmixon	630	Francis	$759

21 Warren, Journals, March 3, 1797; Philadelphia, *Gazette of the United States,* March 4, 1797.
22 Philadelphia *Gazette,* March 18, 1797.
23 Warren, Journals, March 20, 26, 1797. All subsequent citations of box-office receipts are taken from this source.

Darley	510	Prigmore	360
Warren	380	Fox	264
Mr. & Mrs. Byrne	540	Mrs. Francis	325[24]

Harwood, the comedian, was the only actor whose benefit receipts exceeded hers. In addition to being "a great favorite," he had the advantage of the first Chestnut Street theatre performance of *Werter* with Moreton, Cooper, and Mrs. Merry playing leading roles. The benefits continued until May 6, when the theatre closed in order to resume its activities in Baltimore before a June 10 deadline. After that date a new city council prohibited theatre performances in Baltimore until October 10 each year.[25] Before the initiation of the Baltimore season, Warren briefly evaluated the 1796–1797 Philadelphia season concluding that the company was "very strong"; he also noted his reservations and commendations for a few actors, including Mrs. Merry: "Byrnes' Ballets got out in a very great style—but the audience did not like Mrs. Byrnes [sic] exhibiting her legs and frequently hips &—she was obliged to lengthen her petticoats—Mrs. Merry made a great impression—Cooper was well received when he took any sort of pains. Moreton a great favorite Harwood also—."[26]

Within ten days of the Philadelphia closing, the company had made the overnight journey to Baltimore and opened the intense four-week engagement consisting of the most successful productions of the Philadelphia season. Anne played in almost every performance, appearing in eighteen of twenty-one presentations. In order to take maximum advantage of the brief engagement, the company played every night except Sunday, an especially grueling schedule for only two of the shows were presented a second time. The actors doubled on benefits and the Merry-Moreton was first. Once again Anne Merry tried to help her husband's career by selecting his farce *The Enchanted Flute* as the evening's afterpiece. The only benefit to exceed the Merry-Moreton night of $518 was the Harwood-Oldmixon benefit, which earned $617. At

[24] *Ibid.*, March 29–May 6, 1797; July 5–7, 1797.
[25] *Ibid.*, June 11, 1797.
[26] *Ibid.*, May 6, 1797.

the end of the benefits the theatre remained dark for a night in preparation for *Columbus,* "got out with the same splendour as in Philadelphia as far as the Theatre would admit." The spectacular's success in Baltimore equalled its Philadelphia reception, bringing in $999.87, the largest receipts of the engagement. Although the managers waited a fortnight for an answer to their petition to extend the Baltimore season, the city council ("a set of stony hearted villians [*sic*]") rejected the request; whereupon Mrs. Merry returned with the rest of the company to Philadelphia for a brief five-night engagement. Wignell, fearful of Fourth of July festivities and riots, postponed the opening until July 5.[27] The response to the brief run of two stock nights and two benefits must have been discouraging because box office receipts never exceeded $325.

With the Baltimore theatre closed until October, the Philadelphia summer theatre business extremely slow, and the threat of yellow fever bound to make theatre patrons even scarcer, Anne may have anticipated relief from her heavy performance schedule. But Wignell soon arranged for an invasion of New York dramatic territory, abandoned for the summer by its winter occupants, the Old American Company. More than a month elapsed after the close of the Philadelphia theatre before the Merrys journeyed to New York in a chartered stagecoach with several members of the company.[28] Wignell's plans included a refurbishment of Rickett's Circus in Greenwich Street for twelve performances. But partly because of the extended yellow fever epidemic in Philadelphia, the Chestnut Street company embarked on a demanding three-month engagement. Although most of the forty-six performances were revivals from the Philadelphia and Baltimore seasons, Wignell offered few plays as many as three times. In Mrs. Merry's thirty-one appearances she enacted twenty-one different characterizations, four of them new to her. The New York visit must have been an exhausting one, but it must have been pleasurable as well, for it gave Anne the opportunity to

27 *Ibid.,* June 11, July 5, 1797.
28 *Ibid.,* August 17, 1797.

share the stage again with two new company members, former Covent Garden stage-mates John Bernard[29] and James Fennell. As Goldfinch in *The Road to Ruin*, Bernard joined Mrs. Merry on the American boards the second night of the New York engagement.[30] Within the next two weeks James Fennell's appearance as Zanga in Edward Young's *Revenge* gave her the opportunity to play opposite him once again as Leonora.

If the New York engagement brought together old acquaintances, it also brought Mrs. Merry the challenge of the seemingly ubiquitous Kemble talents. On August 30, Mrs. Whitlock, sister to Mrs. Siddons and John Kemble, joined the rival theatrical forces at the John Street Theatre under the management of Monsieur Sollee of the Charleston theatre. Originally engaged by Wignell as the leading actress of the Chestnut Street company in 1793, Mrs. Whitlock had become noted for her performances of the roles of Lady Macbeth, Imogen, Belvidera, Calista, Euphrasia, and Monimia. In 1796 she and her actor-husband left Wignell's company and subsequently played one of America's first starring engagements in Boston before joining Sollee's company in Charleston.[31] In 1797, from the time of Mrs. Whitlock's ar-

[29] Robert Merry greeted Bernard with a characteristic pun when he arrived in New York to join the Chestnut Street company. "Ah, John, have you come to make your fortune like the rest of us? I'm afraid," shrugging his shoulders, "you'll be a bit." "I plead guilty," said I; "but what in the name of Mammon tempted you—you, that I've heard so often say you could never live in America?" "Nonsense, John," he replied, "you know that I always liked to be in A-merry-key." John Bernard, *Retrospections of America, 1797–1811*, ed. Laurence Hutton and Brander Matthews (New York, 1887), 49.

[30] The Bernard-Merry friendship had opportunity for further renewal when Bernard became ill after his second American performance. "After the first treatment the doctor ordered me to go immediately into the country and to take brandy-and-water. This was no disagreeable prescription; I fixed on the little Dutch village of Haerlem for my retreat, and Robert Merry's joy at having met with me was so great that he insisted on sharing my rustication, remarking, in his old way, 'it was not the first time he had found it a pleasure to cheer me.' When thus together we had so much to remember, discuss, reply to, propose, and project, that we sat up night after night, administering plentifully the doctor's elixir, till in a few days I found myself completely restored, having experienced, perhaps, the pleasantest cure upon record." *Ibid.*, 50.

[31] See Mary Ruth Michael, "A History of the Professional Theatre in Boston from the Beginning to 1816" (Ph. D. dissertation, Radcliffe College, 1941), 140.

rival in New York on August 27 until her departure in early October, comparisons of the two actresses and two companies were no doubt a source of much theatrical discussion. In versatility Mrs. Merry undoubtedly had the advantage for she played in comic, pathetic, and tragic roles; whereas Mrs. Whitlock confined her appearances to tragic parts, many of them staples in Anne's repertoire. During the month of parallel engagements, Anne portrayed such tragic roles as Belvidera, Calista, Leonora, Juliet, and Desdemona, while Mrs. Whitlock appeared as Isabella, Horatia, Lady Randolph, and Euphrasia.[32] Inevitably the fortunes of the two actresses were bound to those of their respective companies. The week before the arrival of Mrs. Whitlock, the inferior Charleston company recorded the low box-office receipts of $130 and $80, while the much stronger Wignell forces earned as much as $734 and $413. Mrs. Whitlock's initial New York performance increased John Street Theatre receipts to $280, but even her well-established reputation and talents could not overcome the attraction of Mrs. Merry, whose performances were powerfully supported by Moreton, Cooper, Fennell, and Bernard. As Dunlap foresaw, Sollee and his company soon "ran aground," withdrawing from New York by the first week in October.[33] After the retreat of the John Street forces Wignell's company commanded the New York theatrical scene until the yellow fever abated enough to allow a return to Philadelphia.

During the New York engagement, Anne also encountered the competition of Mrs. Marshall, the other actress with whom her performance of Juliet had been compared in Philadelphia. Both Mrs. Marshall and her husband had left Wignell's troupe in 1796 for an engagement with the Boston company but had rejoined it in New York September 22. Prior to her departure from Philadelphia and prior to Mrs. Merry's arrival, Mrs. Marshall had performed roles which were also standard in Anne's repertoire: Sophia,

[32] George C. D. Odell, *Annals of the New York Stage* (New York, 1927–49), I, 450–72.

[33] William Dunlap, *Diary of William Dunlap*, (New York, 1930), I, 139–41, 147.

Juliet, Amanthis, Indiana, and Emily Tempest. As leading actresses at the Chestnut Street theatre, Mrs. Marshall and Mrs. Whitlock had shared leading roles. Mrs. Whitlock restricted herself to tragic parts, while Mrs. Marshall dominated the comic and pathetic roles as well as the gentler tragic characterizations such as Desdemona, Ophelia, and Juliet. When Mrs. Marshall rejoined Wignell's company, rather than meeting as rivals from competing theatre ensembles, Mrs. Marshall and Mrs. Merry confronted each other as members of the same company. Although both actresses were versatile and could play some of the same roles, they were basically suited to different kinds of parts: Mrs. Marshall was the beau ideal of comic romps and Anne the new standard of tragic excellence. One of their first notable appearances together occurred in New York in October when they performed in Elizabeth Inchbald's *Everyone Has His Fault.* Mrs. Marshall played the young Edward long separated from his mother, Lady Eleanor Irwin, portrayed by Anne. The scene in which Edward recognizes his mother almost by instinct and chooses to remain with her instead of his grandfather subsequently became one of the most memorable moments in Chestnut Street theatre history. Durang recalled: "The impressiveness of the affecting scene . . . drew tears from the most enlightened audience . . . and well we remember it was the theme of conversation in every circle the next day."[34] It soon became evident that the combination of their talents was a powerful addition to Wignell's company.

Detailed accounts of Anne's New York performances are not available, but sizable box office receipts indicate that she was a key attraction of the Philadelphia company. Her benefit, shared with Fennell, was the only one which "succeeded," each of them earning two hundred dollars. Enthusiastic public approval is further substantiated by a critic's comment, "In the praises of Mrs. Merry we do but echo the public voice." William Dunlap, cautious in his praise, recorded a few personal reactions to her per-

---

[34] Durang, "The Philadelphia Stage," Chap. XXI, September 24, 1854.

formances: he noted that in *Venice Preserv'd* she made a "lasting impression"; he regarded her Desdemona as "enchanting"; and he viewed her Juliet "with much delight."[35] Although the Chestnut Street forces never invaded New York again, Anne made such an indelible impression that on four future occasions she returned to New York for starring engagements.

The conclusion of the New York engagement on November 25 ended the first year of Mrs. Merry's American theatrical career. It was a year of hard work and significant accomplishment. She gave approximately one hundred and two performances of thirty-one roles, enlarging her repertoire by eighteen characterizations. As in the British Isles, she channeled her energies into pathetic and comic roles, as well as tragic, with most effort given to the comic and pathetic. The heavy schedule and the extensive scope of the repertoire, in breadth and depth, rigorously tested her endurance for American theatre demands. No doubt previous summer tours of the English provinces prepared her to meet this test, but the schedule must have occasionally taken its toll on the actress's health: Warren noted several cancellations of performances because of Mrs. Merry's illnesses. In addition to confronting the heavy demands of the American repertoire, Anne established a new standard of acting excellence in three major American cities. From the night of her first American performance her acting "exceeded prediction" and "furnished a new standard of excellence." Because her acting was judged within the framework of the strongest theatrical company in the United States, her superior position takes on increased significance. Moreover, when competition with Mrs. Whitlock and Mrs. Marshall enlarged that framework of evaluation, her ability emerges in even bolder relief. In one arduous year she established both her versatility and her artistic superiority. As she began her second year at the Chestnut Street theatre, that company could well boast of possessing the finest actress in the United States, "without rival in America."[36]

[35] Odell, *Annals of the New York Stage*, I, 466; Dunlap, *Diary*, I, 138, 150, 144.
[36] Philadelphia, *Gazette of the United States*, December 21, 1796.

IV

Mrs. Merry Becomes a Star

1797-1801

With the additional company strength of the Bernards and the Marshalls, Anne Brunton Merry embarked on her second year in the United States with one of the strongest contingents of actors with whom she ever worked in America. Unfortunately, when James Fennell rejoined the company in January, she lost the support of Thomas Cooper, who broke his contract and abandoned Philadelphia for New York, where his talents might develop without competition from Fennell.[1] The loss of Cooper was perhaps the first portent of a troubled year for Mrs. Merry, as well as the company. In terms of performances the year was less strenuous, for she made approximately 87 appearances compared with 102 of the year before. She played almost the same number of characterizations as the previous year, thirty-one, thirteen of them new. Her most frequently performed role was that of the giddy, irresponsible, but eventually reformed Miss Dorillon of Elizabeth Inchbald's *Wives as They Were and Maids as They Are*. Anne portrayed this role with such "tender eloquence" that it was not unusual "to behold in the lofty tiers of boxes, the ladies wiping from their eyes sentimental offerings."[2]

Within the same month she initiated one of the most auspicious series of performances of her career by appearing with Fennell for the first time before Philadelphia audiences in *The Revenge*. Recruited by Wignell in 1793 as the leading tragic actor for the Chestnut Street theatre, Fennell had already established

---

1 Warren, Journals, January 20, 1798.
2 Philadelphia *Gazette*, December 19, 1797.

himself as a great favorite with playgoers. But his genius could not reconcile with his many interests (in particular, saltmaking), extravagant tastes, and exceptional acting ability. His erratic performance pattern damaged his relations with managers, frequently deprived Anne of a leading actor worthy of her ability, and eventually crippled the fulfillment of his own talents. However, in January, 1797, after he had been absent three years from Philadelphia, "boxes . . . crowded with the first people in the city" and "repeated and constant applauses of the audience" welcomed his return in his famous characterization of Zanga. The applause was no doubt also meant for Mrs. Merry and Moreton, who it was "taken for granted . . . were not deficient."[3] Several days later another full house approved a presentation of *Othello* so successful that one critic proclaimed "no play of Shakespeare's was ever performed in America with greater applause . . . or received with greater justice (with a few exceptions) from the exertions of the performers." Tributes went to Anne, whose portrayal of Desdemona "was all that could be wished, all that could be expected from this accomplished actress. This then is complete praise, for who ever saw Mrs. Merry that was not charmed?"[4]

Fennell and Anne appeared next in *Columbus*, performed especially for Little Turtle, an Indian chief.[5] On two other occasions during the spring Anne played for "special dignitaries": *Romeo and Juliet* was presented "by particular desire, and for the entertainment of the Chiefs of the Wyandot Indians," and *Isabella* was performed "by desire of President John Adams."

Fennell's availability accounts for the large number of tragic roles which Anne performed that spring. He made it possible for her to exhibit the full range of her tragic repertoire. In addition to Leonora, Isabella, Juliet, and Desdemona, she enacted Calista, Belvidera, Gertrude, Roxana, Cordelia, Monimia, and—for the first time in America—Horatia. In early February she added a

[3] Philadelphia, *Gazette of the United States,* January 4, 1798.
[4] Philadelphia, *Porcupine's Gazette,* January 13, 1798.
[5] Warren, Journals, January 10, 1798.

new role to this list by originating the part of Eloisa in *Fenelon; or the Nuns of Cambray*, probably "altered from a celebrated French play," which Merry had translated in England.[6] According to Bernard, the drama was put together by the combined energies of the Merrys and himself. He remembered that his "old pupil and stagemate, Mrs. Merry, drew out the plot, I wrote the lighter parts, and Merry the love-scenes."[7] The collaboration won sufficient approval from Wignell to produce the work. He even took "Fennell out of jail to play the principal character but this gentleman's system of living being of a nature which threatened him hourly with a fresh arrest, Merry remarked, 'It's Fennell-on to-night; it will be Fennell-off in the morning;' and, much to our chagrin, the pun was a prophecy." Supported by Mrs. Merry, Fennell, and Mrs. Marshall, the new drama attracted a crowded house of noisy spectators, disinterested "during the whole of the first act, in which no male character appeared." Bernard implies that their "darling play, which babe-like, had just opened its eyes, smiled on the world, and died," was not successful.[8] Despite these words, records show that Wignell scheduled the work five times in Philadelphia that year, twice in Baltimore, and once in Annapolis, for a total of eight performances, which might be termed at least a moderate success by prevailing standards.

In February the closing of the theatre for a week interrupted Mrs. Merry's schedule, as well as that of the entire company. The managers announced the action was necessary because of a combination of circumstances: the "defection of Cooper . . . the bad conduct of Fennell [who refused to play Castalio because he was not given sufficient notice] and the sickness of Moreton." After the theatre reopened, Mrs. Merry resumed an intense program, learning six new characterizations before the playhouse closed in early May. In the first benefit of the season, theatregoers crowded the house at an early hour for Anne's first appearance as Lady

[6] Philadelphia, *Gazette of the United States*, February 1, 1798.

[7] Bernard, *Retrospections of America*, 72.

[8] *Ibid.*, 72–73; Philadelphia *Gazette*, February 3, 1798; Bernard, *Retrospections of America*, 73.

Teazle in Sheridan's *School for Scandal.* She portrayed the famous character with "taste and elegance but was too imperfect in the part to give it that spirit and effect which it required—." The same evening, she made one of her rare appearances in an after-piece as Cowslip in *The Agreeable Surprise.* Obviously aware of her musical inadequacies, she "came forward . . . with all the apparent timidity of a theatrical *debut."* Because of her embarrassment her voice was "feeble and unimpressive"; nevertheless, she was loudly applauded as she managed to win her audience "by charms that no music can equal, and that receive the highest polish of their expression from beauty, virtue and simplicity."[9] On March 30 Anne and Fennell headed the company in a benefit performance of *The Roman Father* for the gravely ill Moreton. Although the benefit brought eight hundred dollars, nothing could save his life and he died of consumption on April 2. His was not only a "never replaced"[10] loss to the entire company, but probably a keen personal loss to Mrs. Merry, who had shared with him many American performances. The theatre closed for three days in tribute to the actor and a month later it closed for the season.

By May 18 Anne and a severely depleted company resumed their theatrical activities in Baltimore. As Warren noted in his journal, during the Philadelphia season the company had lost three of its principal actors: "Moreton—by death, Cooper by desertion . . . Fennell—went to make salt."[11] Thus divested of tragic support, during the sixteen-night engagement Mrs. Merry divided her energies more evenly between her comic and tragic repertoire. Having received from Baltimore officials a negative reply to a request to extend the season, Wignell selected Annapolis as the site of his next campaign.

The sixteen miles between Annapolis and Baltimore may not have seemed a strenuous move to actors who had learned their

[9] Durang, "The Philadelphia Stage," Chap. XXX, October 26, 1854; Philadelphia *Gazette,* March 22, 1798.
[10] Bernard, *Retrospections of America,* 268.
[11] Warren, Journals, May 4, 1798.

art on comparable tours of English provinces, for some walked the distance rather than pay for transportation. Warren "set off to walk to Annapolis" but "the day so hot—we could not reach it until next morning." If, as Bernard declared, Annapolis was "The Bath of America," containing "a concentration of the best of Philadelphia and Virginian society," it was not a society hungry for theatricals. In the sweltering summer of 1798 even "the oldest residents . . . [did] not remember any summer so oppressive."[12]

Box-office receipts, ranging from a high of $364 to a low of $51, register the disastrous effects of the weather on playgoing. Of the performances in Annapolis, only eleven earned as much as $150. Such low receipts forced Mrs. Merry and the rest of the company temporarily to receive wages according to the sharing system rather than by salary. As early as August 11 the futility of keeping the theatre open prompted the company treasurer Samuel Anderson to propose that the company "suspend performances until the weather . . . shall become more moderate." Bernard, acting manager in the absence of Wignell, decided to keep the theatre open, however, while Anderson went to Baltimore to raise more cash. Finally, when Wignell returned on August 27, he closed the theatre for ten days. It may have been during this time that Bernard, with all the resourcefulness of a provincial thespian, decided "to divide the company and make lecturing excursions to the smaller towns, an experiment which had been often tried before under similar circumstances." Warren, leading a division which included Mrs. Merry and four other performers, headed for "North of Maryland and Virginia."[13] Warren did not record the excursions, but Bernard's account of his foray into Delaware gives insight into the type of journey Mrs. Merry may have experienced.

Armed with letters of recommendation, Bernard and his contingent of actor-lecturers hired a sloop and visited several small

[12] *Ibid.*, June 30, 1798; Bernard, *Retrospections of America*, 84; Warren, Journals, August 27, 1798.
[13] Warren, Journals, August 11, 1798; Bernard, *Retrospections of America*, 116.

towns on the eastern side of the Chesapeake Bay. At Chesterton they sang and recited in an Assembly Room before about twenty curious paying customers and twice as many nonpaying onlookers crowded at the doorway. Undaunted by the meager attendance, the actors serenaded about the town later the same night, "flattering themselves that if the women—the most influential part of all communities—once heard their voices, the next evening our room would be as packed as the 'Black Hole.' The compliment was so novel in the quiet streets of this secluded place that every window flew up and some score of female faces popped out, which was considered a favorable omen. But the Delaware maidens were better calculators; the next night we performed to only ten dollars." It soon became clear that the pleasure of the excursion "began to overbalance its profit, and like more eminent commanders, I was compelled with chagrin, to give the signal for retreat."[14] With yellow fever still raging in New York and Philadelphia and the company prohibited from playing in Baltimore until October 1, the actors had little alternative except to resume performances in Annapolis on September 7. If Mrs. Merry and her fellow actors suffered the severe financial consequences of the yellow fever epidemic, they also must have felt its grief-laden repercussions when it struck within their families. Such must have been the case when Anderson received word on September 8 that his twenty-two-year-old son had died in New York.[15]

A doubtless saddened, impoverished, but generous company gave a benefit performance for the "Sick and Poor of Philadelphia" on September 17 in Annapolis. The $205 earned exceeded all of the actor benefits which began the following week. For these benefits, the performer whose name was advertised received receipts in excess of $150.[16] Thus, Anne's receipts of $152 enriched the actress by only $2. The small margin of profit indicates a distressing financial situation for her, but it was one shared by

14 Bernard, *Retrospections of America*, 116–17.
15 Warren Journals, September 8, 1798.
16 *Ibid.*, September 28, 1798.

the entire company. Only the Byrnes' benefit exceeded Mrs. Merry's, with a profit of eight dollars.

After remaining in Annapolis long enough to avoid the turbulent election week, the company returned to Baltimore for the "autumn campaign," which "liberally compensated for . . . summer losses" and allowed the managers to return to the salary system. But now, instead of financial problems, widespread illness plagued the company. Mrs. Merry was one of the few who evaded the sick list that fall. While she engaged in her regular routine of performing, she also found time to encourage a fledgling actor, William B. Wood, who later became manager of the Chestnut Street theatre. Wood, who had made his acting debut the preceding summer, gratefully accepted help from the Merrys, who were "kind and encouraging, pointing out some of my most prominent faults, while they promised me future counsel." Anne gave Wood further support in his Baltimore debut. For the occasion Wood says he played with the confidence that "Mrs. Merry . . . will aid me with her advice, as well as conceal some of my defects by her skill and care."[17]

In addition to helping the young neophyte, she continued to encourage and assist her husband in his playwriting. In fact, the night before the forty-three-year-old Merry suffered a fatal stroke, she was looking over a new manuscript he hoped to submit to Thomas Harris at Covent Garden. Bernard remembered that upon returning from a visit with a friend, Merry had found his wife engrossed in the last act of his play. Deciding not to disturb her, he "took a kiss and his candle and went up to bed. . . . The next morning Merry rose early, apparently quite well, and . . . descending to the garden, where he usually walked before breakfast, met the cook, for whom he had his pun prepared as regularly as she had his coffee. Mrs. Merry came down soon after to complete her revision of the play, and the servant going out to call her husband when the breakfast was ready, found him stretched in the path-

[17] Bernard, *Retrospections of America*, 123; Wood, *Personal Recollections*, 48, 50.

way in a fit of apoplexy." Bernard rushed to the house to find the poet "propped in a chair, tapping his snuffbox and smiling a re-proof at his wife's emotion, while the physicians were holding a consultation in one corner of the room. . . . Three hours after this he breathed his last (and perhaps his only) sigh upon his wife's bosom." Merry's burial two days later, December 26, 1798, in St. Paul's Cemetery, Baltimore, "drew forth the strongest expres-sion of private sympathy"[18] that Bernard had ever witnessed. It seemed to him that "half the population of Maryland walked after the dismal vehicle which now shrouded the sun of our circle." No doubt many strong expressions of sympathy comforted the young widow, but understandably she withdrew to Annapolis for the rest of the Baltimore season.

Mrs. Merry rejoined the company in February when it resumed its usual winter schedule in Philadelphia, where the yellow fever had finally abated. A grieving, fever-riddled city recovering from the loss of an estimated thirty-five hundred victims probably offered little emotional relief to a mourning widow and friends attempting to dispel the "shock and gloom which for many months hung over [their] little circle." Nevertheless Anne im-mediately entered upon an arduous performance schedule by ap-pearing in the season's first production, Thomas Morton's *Secrets Worth Knowing.* The comedy was a keynote for the season, for without male tragic support for Mrs. Merry, Wignell depended upon comedies as the staple attraction. But even a varied sched-ule filled with many new plays could not protect the company from serious financial problems. By the second week in March, the actors were receiving half salaries, and by March 30 the managers were forced to take the "Benefit of the insolvent law." At the same time, the managers assured the actors of fulfilled contracts and that "no difference . . . [would] be made in any one engagement by their insolvency."[19] Anne's financial affairs must

---

[18] Bernard, *Retrospections of America,* 142–44; M. Ray Adams, "Robert Merry and the American Theatre," *Theatre Survey,* VI (May, 1965), 7.
[19] Bernard, *Retrospections of America,* 141; Warren, Journals, March 30, 22, 1799.

have been improved by her benefit on April 1, which totaled $1,160, an amazingly high figure, especially when compared to the next largest benefit total, $889, which Bernard attracted.

The high receipts for Anne's benefit expressed, perhaps, both esteem and sympathy for the young widow. As well as improving her financial situation, her benefit performance of an adaptation (probably Dunlap's) of August von Kotzebue's melodrama *The Stranger* initiated a strenuous series of roles. Mrs. Haller was the first of at least seven new roles the young actress learned in April. Wignell's battery of new works appears to have been a desperate attempt to salvage his disastrous season, while at the same time he also considered finding new audiences. When salaries were further reduced from one-third to one-fourth, he and the company considered moving to Jamaica.[20] Moreover, when William Wood left the company that spring for a commercial career in Jamaica, Wignell asked him to "ascertain whether a short season at Kingston might not be profitable, and give a rest to the audience here."[21]

In the midst of fiscal problems, a demanding schedule, and recovery from the shock of her husband's death, Anne also faced decisions concerning her future. Just as her marriage to Merry had been a turning point in her life and career, so was his untimely death. Marriage to the poet had ultimately brought her to America and now, without him, she considered returning to England. For a time she "resolved to return to Europe, and her arrival in London . . . [was] hourly expected."[22] The important question as to where to continue her career was timely and pertinent. Her original contract with Wignell expired in 1799, leaving her free to return to England. As she considered the possible avenues open to her, she must have realized that she was at a critical point in her career. Now, as she approached her twenty-ninth year, she commanded acting skills, techniques and experi-

[20] Warren, *Journals,* April 20, 1799.
[21] Wood, *Personal Recollections,* 67.
[22] *Monthly Magazine and British Register* (April, 1799), 258.

ence, a knowledge of the scope of her talent, and an emotional range deepened by her recent grief. She was on the brink of her most fruitful years, in which she might experience completely the full potential of her dramatic ability. She probably seriously considered reestablishing a career at Covent Garden, where she might have been a welcome replacement for Mrs. Pope, who had died in 1797. But a return to London would also mean competition once again with the formidable Mrs. Siddons. Even though she may have been confident of her ability to perform within the same sphere as Mrs. Siddons, Anne probably hesitated to forego the advantages of the artistic supremacy she enjoyed in America. This advantage may have become especially evident to her when William Dunlap asked her to join the other prominent American theatre company at the Park Theatre in New York. Dunlap's contract included sixty dollars a week for a season consisting of thirty-four to forty weeks and six hundred dollars insured benefit profits, an especially attractive offer when compared with the fifty-dollars-a-week salary paid to the leading actors of the Park in the season of 1798–1799.[23] Mrs. Merry replied to Dunlap on April 29 that her plans still were not settled:

> Philadelphia, April 29th. 1799
> SIR—In answer to your polite letter, I have to inform you that it is not my intention at present to return to Europe. I am every day in expectation of receiving letters from my connexions in England, and before I know what their wishes are, it will be improper for me to enter into any new engagement.
> Mr. Wignell has invariably behaved to me like a man of honour and a sincere friend; my article with him has in every point been fulfilled to this moment. What the situation of this theatre may be next winter is past conjecture; but I think it *more than probable* that the present holders will still retain the management.
> In the course of the month I think I shall know to a certainty how to proceed in my arrangements for the next season, and will take the earliest opportunity of informing you if any change in this theatre should induce me to leave Philadelphia.

[23] Dunlap, *History of the American Theatre*, II, 111, 70.

Permit me to say, there is no situation on the continent I should accept with greater pleasure than the one offered me in your establishment.

I remain, etc. etc.
ANN [*sic*] MERRY[24]

Regrettably, no further information is available concerning her decision to remain in the United States and with the Chestnut Street theatre. Whatever expected communication she received from England, it did not pull her back to the British Isles, where in all probability her potential financial remuneration was not as great or as certain. Then, too, Thomas Wignell may have influenced her final decision. Enmeshed in a struggle to sustain his company, the manager must have employed all the persuasive means at his disposal to retain such a key attraction as the leading actress in the United States. Anne's ultimate decision to renew her engagement with Wignell in the midst of some of the darkest financial months of the company's history confirms her basic respect for and trust in the manager, which she demonstrated further three and a half years later when she married him.

As the Philadelphia season limped to a close, Anne was once again provided with a leading man. Wignell scheduled Thomson's tragedy *Tancred and Sigismunda* on May 15 in order to introduce Alexander Cain in the character of Tancred opposite her in the role of Sigismunda. The new acquisition made a successful debut, but even though his arrival enabled Wignell to schedule more tragedies in the future, neither the additional actor nor the new spectacular after-piece *Blue Beard* could remedy the company's financial distress. The dismal season created hardships for actors such as William Warren, whose "unmerciful landlord" seized his house while he was at the theatre. Luckily for Warren, the company moved to Baltimore a few nights later and opened the theatre by May 31 for nine performances of seven different plays. As usual Mrs. Merry carried a heavy performance burden during the engagement, portraying six different roles in eight presentations. Because the actors' engagement was brief since

[24] *Ibid.*, 111.

performances were still prohibited between June 10 and October 1, the company returned to the sharing system to assure maximum remuneration for everyone. According to Warren, "performers names . . . [were] put up for benefits and the proceeds to be stocked—and divided equally at the conclusion of the season."[25]

Although the city council passed a bill in favor of Wignell's petition to extend the season, the board of health ("a set of canting thieves") convinced the mayor not to sign it for public health reasons.[26] And Wignell once again searched elsewhere for hospitable summer audiences. While he talked of Lancaster, he attempted a six-night Annapolis run which was eventually extended into an engagement of sixteen performances, thirteen of them plays in which Mrs. Merry carried leading roles. The decision to remain in Annapolis must have been of necessity rather than the result of an unexpected boom in business. In sixteen performances the box-office receipts exceeded two hundred dollars only once and one hundred dollars only four times, and on one occasion receipts fell as low as forty-one dollars. What this meant in actual wages is recorded by Warren, who noted that weekly earnings steadily declined from two dollars per share to as low as fifty cents. Wignell attempted to ease the situation by sending scouts in search of other possible audiences. Bernard and Reinagle reported unfavorably of George Town, as did John Joseph Holland of Lancaster.[27] But when Bernard and Holland undertook a second expedition to the District of Columbia they "returned with the information that they . . . [had] taken the Ball room in George Town." After Holland and Marshall also reported favorably of Easton, southeast of Annapolis across the Chesapeake Bay, the company divided, with half of the troupe going to Easton and the other half to George Town.[28]

Mrs. Merry joined the expedition intended to perform "six plays only" beginning the third week in August, Suter's Tavern,

[25] Warren, Journals, May 26, 31, 1799.
[26] Ibid., June 10, 1799.
[27] Ibid., July 23, 30, 1799.
[28] Ibid., August 3, 10, 1799.

George Town. Records of that engagement are scant, but incomplete newspaper files disclose three play titles advertised, *The Child of Nature*, *The Stranger*, and *The Fair Penitent*. Handicapped by an incomplete company, the thespians scheduled performances which leaned heavily on Anne in leading roles. No doubt the company gave more than three presentations in George Town for they advertised "theatricals" through September 21, after which they announced three additional appearances on the other side of the Potomac "in conjunction with the Alexandria Company."[29] Soon after, the Philadelphia players opened the Baltimore theatre on October 1. Not expecting the Easton forces, Wignell advertised and began the season without them.[30] A full company was on hand for the third performance, however, and by payday, Saturday, October 5, the actors were receiving salaries again. Although no record of the George Town receipts remain, the players probably suffered the usual summer box-office difficulties. The Easton troupe could hardly have fared better, because they had to be financed by an Easton shopkeeper, ask for credit from the captain of the packet boat which carried them across the bay, and collected only $490.25 or $25.50 per share for five weeks of performing.[31] Nevertheless a return to substantial Baltimore box-office receipts did not eliminate other company troubles. The summer had taken a heavy toll: L'Estrange's wife died while he was in Easton and on October 28, "young Henry Warrell" died of fever contracted in Easton. In mid-October, William Warren suffered but survived a severe recurrence of the fever, while Mrs. Merry's illness forced her absence from the boards between October 23 and November 13.[32] She recovered sufficiently to play the seven remaining performances before she returned to Philadelphia for a full "winter campaign."

Anne opened the Chestnut Street theatre season on December 4 in the role of the unfaithful but penitent wife, Mrs. Haller, in

29 Georgetown, *Centinel of Liberty and George-Town and Washington Advertiser*, August 16, September 21, 1799.
30 Warren, Journals, October 1, 1799.
31 *Ibid.*, September 26, 1799; September 19, 1799.
32 *Ibid.*, November 13, 1799.

The Stranger, which had earned as many as eleven performances the previous year. The play, equally popular during 1799–1800, had even achieved earlier successes in London and New York, and Anne found herself once again portraying a characterization made famous by Mrs. Siddons.

The new season had been under way only two weeks when the news of George Washington's death muffled the bells of the city and suspended entertainments for several days. When the theatre reopened it offered mournful decorations and a special program in tribute to one of its most distinguished and loyal supporters. Wignell spoke a monody, the orchestra played music which Reinagle composed for the occasion, and the company performed *The Roman Father,* identified with Washington because of its patriotic sentiments.[33]

As the company resumed its normal schedule on December 28, Anne began a series of appearances in sentimental comedies. Yet this season her repertoire differed from the previous year in two ways: she performed in many translated plays by a single playwright, Kotzebue, and she once again acted many of her most noted tragic roles. During this season of 1799–1800 the company did at least eight plays translated from the works of Kotzebue. Anne performed in two of his popular holdovers from the previous year, *Lovers' Vows* and *The Stranger.* In addition, of the six new Kotzebue presentations, she played leading roles in five: *The Reconciliation* or *The Birth-Day, The Count of Burgundy, False Shame, Sighs,* and *Pizarro.* She appeared most frequently (ten times) in *The Reconciliation* that year and almost as often in two other Kotzebue plays, *The Stranger* (nine times) and *Pizarro* (eight times). As adapted by Richard B. Sheridan, *Pizarro* was performed in Philadelphia for the first time for Wignell's benefit late in the season. He probably anticipated the enthusiastic reception for the melodrama, which had won thirty-one consecutive London presentations as performed by Charles Kemble, John Kemble, Sarah Siddons, and Dorothy Jordan. In Philadelphia,

[33] Durang, "The Philadelphia Stage," Chap. XXXII, December 10, 1854.

newspapers advertised new scenery, dresses, decorations, music, processions, and a description of the most spectacular scenes, attracting such large audiences that the play was given four successive Philadelphia performances, extending the season an extra night.[34]

The dominance of Kotzebue's works in the repertoire reflects the growing popularity of the playwright who became so well identified with the dramatic form, melodrama. While these thrilling plays provided Anne with many new vehicles, they offered no appreciable new challenge to her because the heroines of melodrama do not differ markedly from the pathetic young ladies of late eighteenth century sentimental comedies prominent in her repertory since her days at Covent Garden. For example, Emma, the essence of filial affection, tender emotion, and arch simplicity in *The Reconciliation,* is similar to previously portrayed heroines of comparable virtues such as Amanthis in *The Child of Nature.* And although the young widow's ability to portray tender characterizations continued to make her a decided asset to the company, the roles obviously did not enlarge the scope of her powers. Not until the return of Thomas Cooper to the company on March 21 was she able to renew a series of tragic roles and attempt three new Shakespearean heroines.

Cooper's reappearance with the Philadelphia company was the consequence of the long-protected lawsuit Wignell and Reinagle had brought against him for breach of contract in 1798. When it was finally settled in the spring of 1800, Cooper not only lost his case and had to pay a judgment of more than £500, plus interests and costs,[35] but he also found himself in difficulty with his New York manager Dunlap. When the young actor left New York to attend to the suit in March, 1800, he obtained leave from the Park Theatre; however, his affairs in Philadelphia detained him longer than the stipulated length of time. As a result of a subsequent controversy with Dunlap, Cooper withdrew from

[34] Philadelphia, *Gazette of the United States,* May 12, 19, 1800.
[35] Warren, Journals, March 17, 1800.

the New York company and resumed his position in the Chestnut Street company, appearing there for the first time in two years as Pierre in *Venice Preserv'd*.[36] To take advantage of Cooper's talent, Wignell next scheduled *The Wheel of Fortune* and *Romeo and Juliet*. Rather than immediately revive additional stock pieces, the manager devoted the first half of April to new works, undoubtedly putting a considerable strain on Mrs. Merry, who in that month presented nine new roles. One of the most spectacular of these was that of Angela in M. G. Lewis' thrilling melodrama *The Castle Spectre*. Here, the exciting climax calls for the sudden appearance of the ghost of Elvina, enabling her daughter Angela to plunge a dagger into the heart of the villain. For her benefit on April 14 Anne portrayed Amelia in Kotzebue's *False Shame* and for the after-piece ("for that night only"), performed for the first time the role of Yarico in Colman's perenially favorite comic opera *Inkle and Yarico*.[37] Her efforts were appreciated so enthusiastically that she earned $1,330, one of the greatest amounts that she ever received for a benefit. The only other benefit that spring approximating the amount was Wignell's which coincided with the first performance of *Pizarro*, May 14, and brought $1,202 into the box office.

During the other benefit performances Anne added three new Shakespearean roles to her repertoire. The first, Lady Percy, must have been learned hurriedly for Warren's benefit on April 19, when he substituted *Henry IV* for *King John* at the request of "Mrs. Lyton, Lady of the British Minister."[38] Two nights later Anne enacted the role of Constance in *King John* and in the same week instead of portraying Gertrude for the first revival of *Hamlet* in two years, she gave her initial performance as Ophelia.

By May 23 the company began a sixteen-performance Baltimore run, giving the young actress ten appearances. As usual, the city ordinance prevented presentations after June 10, when the

[36] *Ibid.*, March 21, 1800.
[37] Philadelphia, *Gazette of the United States*, April 14, 1800.
[38] Warren, Journals, April 19, 1800.

company divided once again for the summer months. Although Warren recorded that he, Francis, Blissett, and Tom Warrell[39] took a packet boat to Cambridge to give several performances, as well as to play in Easton, Annapolis, Queen Anne, and Upper Marlboro, it is not known where Anne spent the rest of June and July. She, with other members of the company, may have remained in Baltimore until Wignell collected his actors in August for the opening of the first theatre in the new federal capital emerging on the banks of the Potomac.

Under the provision of a law enacted in July, 1790, the Congress was scheduled to convene in the new Federal City in December, 1800. The removal of government offices from Philadelphia began in May and by July 6 executive departments had been transferred to the new capital. Hoping "to obtain footing in Washington, where he might keep together his company during the summer, in the event of a recurrence of pestilence," Wignell accepted a request to establish a theatre in the new city.[40] Although as early as June 17 he and Holland visited the new raw capital and consulted with Dr. William Thornton, the district commissioner and the architect of the national Capitol and the White House, the theatre was not ready until August.[41] Instead of trying to build a new playhouse, Wignell converted a building "nearly in the centre of the new metropolis" designed but never occupied as a hotel. (In later years the building housed the federal Post Office Department and the United States Patent Office.) "It consisted of a large spacious centre building, with two extensive wings. The former was offered by the proprietors as an eligible structure for . . . [Wignell's] purpose.[42] By August 7 members of the company began arriving and settling at Mrs. Finch's

[39] According to Warren, however, Tom Warrell left them July 24, 1800. Warren's Journal also reveals that the company had given up their salaries for the Warrell family benefit in Baltimore, probably as a farewell gesture since they were returning to England. Warren commented additionally, "Wignell is very glad . . . the Old Folks are only an incumbrance." June 2, 1800.

[40] Wood, *Personal Recollections*, 55–56.

[41] "Diary of Mrs. William Thornton, 1800–1863," *Records of the Columbia Historical Society*, X (1907), 156.

[42] Wood, *Personal Recollections*, 55.

at Greenleaf's Point for five dollars per week.[43] Wignell went to Baltimore on August 9 to collect the rest of the company, but the opening of "The United States Theatre" suffered delay. "On the way to Washington a furious storm of rain invaded the wagons, and drenched the tasteful labors of the [scenic] painters so seriously as it made it necessary to repaint nearly the whole." Finally, on a warm Friday, August 22, 1800, Wignell, Cooper, and Mrs. Merry, leading the company in a performance of *Venice Preserv'd*, opened the first theatre in Washington. The production was "warmly received and applauded by an audience, more numerous, as well as splendid, than can be conceived from a population so slender and so scattered."[44] No doubt the distinguished audience included such notables as Thomas Law, writer of the special prologue spoken by Wignell and wealthy English resident of Washington, who married Eliza Parke Custis, granddaughter of Martha Washington.[45] Wood's assertion that the "encouragement continued to exceed his expectations, yet fell very far below his [Wignell's] expenditure," is substantiated by Warren's record that box-office receipts exceeded two hundred dollars only four times during the sixteen performances, and once, fell as low as forty-three dollars.[46]

Perhaps the "principal performers" felt somewhat compensated by the "gratifying attention and hospitality" offered them by the citizens of Washington. According to Wood, "Many . . . commenced at this period acquaintances and friendships which have continued with unabated kindness through a long course of succeeding years." Washington ladies who extended courtesies to Anne Merry included Mrs. William Thornton, daughter of the prominent Brodeau family of Philadelphia and wife of the district commissioner. On Tuesday, September 2, Mrs. Thornton wrote in her diary: "–drank tea & then took Mrs. Ray with us to visit Mrs. Merry who lodges with some of the other Players at the

[43] Warren, Journals, August 8, 1800.
[44] Wood, *Personal Recollections*, 55, 56.
[45] Deering Davis, Stephen Dorsey, and Ralph Hall, *Georgetown Houses of the Federal Period, 1780–1830* (Cornwall, N. Y., 1944),22.
[46] Wood, *Personal Recollections*, 56.

Point—None of the Ladies who visited her last year from George Town have been to see her—and very few come to the Plays."[47] Mrs. Thornton does not reveal why the George Town ladies were at the time neither calling on the actress nor attending the plays. No doubt distance and summer heat had much to do with it, but Mrs. Thornton offered hospitality to the actress on several occasions: "Friday 12th [September]. . . . After dinner Dr. T. . . . returned just in time to accompany us to the play—It was Columbus & Fortune's frolic.—There were about 300 persons a full house for this place.—The Scenery was much better than I expected, & it was altogether very entertaining. Got home about ½ after eleven. Lent our carriage to Mrs. Merry to go home in."[48] At the same time, Mrs. Merry's professional duties limited her social activities, as Mrs. Thornton indicated: "Sunday 14 [September] very warm Just as I had done dressing Mrs. Murry [sic] & Mr. Reinagle called—invited them to tea on Tuesday next but she said she shou'd be so much engaged in preparing to act the part of Elvira in Pizarro that she did not think she shou'd be able to come." As Anne predicted, she was not able to free herself from the theatre for tea: when Mrs. Thornton returned from a visit to the "President's House" she found "that our Carriage which I had sent for Mrs. Merry had returned empty she cou'd not come.—" On the following evening Mrs. Thornton evaluated the results of the preparations for *Pizarro*: "Went to the theatre very early expecting to get a good seat, but all the front ones in the boxes being engaged we went into the highest row in the Pit.—. . . . Everybody seemed to be pleased.—we got home before twelve."[49]

But Mrs. Thornton was not always so favorably impressed by what she saw at the theatre, as other reports reveal.

Friday 29th [August]
Dressed to go to the Play, tho' I had a headache & pain in my Jaws.—We walked there about six O'clock–There was a very

[47] *Ibid.*, "Diary of Mrs. William Thornton," 186.
[48] "Diary of Mrs. William Thornton," 190.
[49] *Ibid.*, 191–92.

Anne Brunton at fifteen

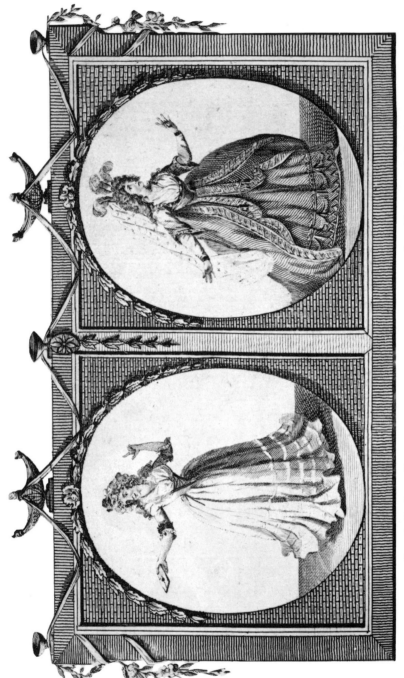

Dorothy Jordan as Peggy
in *The Country Girl*

Anne Brunton as Euphrasia
in *The Grecian Daughter*

George Holman and Anne Brunton
as Romeo and Juliet

Anne Brunton as Calista in
The Fair Penitent

Robert Merry

Thomas Wignell

William Warren

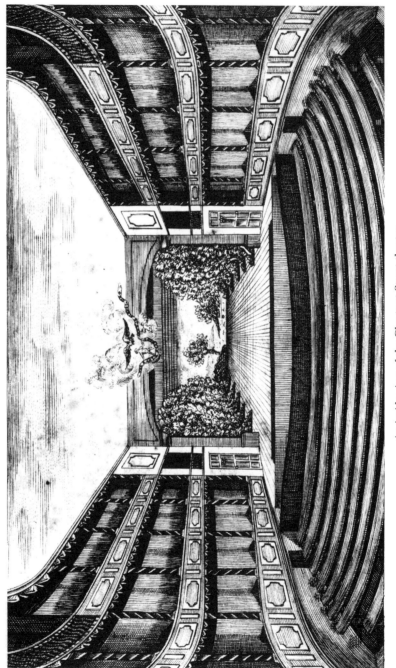

An inside view of the Chestnut Street theatre

A portrait of Anne Brunton made
after her marriage to William Warren

A portrait of Anne Brunton made while she was
the wife of Thomas Wignell

thin house, & the Characters excepting two or three were badly supported it was altogether very dull.—It was as good as a sermon The wheel of fortune by Cumberland—Mrs. Merry was sick & another obliged to take the part she ought to have acted to do the piece justice.—

.   .   .   .

Friday 19th [September] . . . About five O'clock Mr. T. Peter called, he staid 'till he found he detained us from going to the Play—but we need not have been in a hurry for the house was a very thin one—the night before they had only about 40—The Play was a "Cure for the heartache" by Mrs. [sic] Thos. Moreton.—It was rather dull. Take it all in all you may see it's like again.—[50]

The young matron leaves little doubt that for her, and probably for many other playgoers, the enjoyment of the performance often depended on the appearance of the company's leading actress. On September 6, when Mrs. Thornton discovered that Mrs. Merry would not perform that evening, she prepared to go to the farm instead.[51]

By the close of the Washington engagement on September 20, the appearance of yellow fever in Baltimore convinced the managers to open their fall season in Philadelphia. On the trip Anne shared a hired stage with Warren, Morris, Wood, and Wignell, who engaged the vehicle and paid the expenses of the journey.[52] Reports of the fever in Baltimore had become so alarming that the players chose a much longer route to Philadelphia to avoid the contaminated city. The rainy seven-day journey by way of Frederick, York, and Lancaster was lengthened by the illness of Mrs. Merry, whose indisposition delayed the travelers all day at York and extra time at Lancaster.[53] However, by October 1, the players arrived safely in Philadelphia and began preparations for the opening, October 7, "For the Benefit of the Sick and Poor of Baltimore."

Anne embarked upon her fifth year at the Chestnut Street

[50] Ibid., 185, 193–94.
[51] Ibid., 188.
[52] Warren, Journals, September 8, 25, October 1, 1800.
[53] Ibid., September 28, September 29, 1800.

theatre with a company which Dunlap admits, "ranked higher than that of New York."[54] Cooper, Bernard, and Wood (returned from the West Indies) provided key male support and two young actresses, Ellen and Juliana Westray (afterward known as Mrs. John Darley and Mrs. William Wood) relieved Mrs. Merry of some of the younger pathetic roles which did not demand the skills of the busy actress.

The presence of Cooper again allowed the young widow to appear in at least eleven tragedies, although for the most part she did not alter her repertoire pattern noticeably from the previous year. Her excellence, so well established and acclaimed, prompted one critic to comment: "We can add nothing to the rich exchequer of the fame of the first rate actress. The language of praise is trite to this lady."[55] Tributes began early in the season when, as Juliet, Mrs. Merry gave a "luminous and unbroken display of [her] powers." In every scene the actress presented something to admire: "The tenderness and feeling with which the balcony scene was sustained, were only equalled by the terror and the distraction of that in the chamber, where her affrighted imagination depicted the horrors of the ghastly sepulchre."[56] A few nights later she played Elvira (*Pizarro*), a woman seduced by the glory of the victorious Spanish conqueror.[57] Disillusioned by his inhumanity, however, she assists his enemy Rolla to escape and arms him to assassinate the sleeping Pizarro. Rolla, unable to carry out the treachery, awakens the sleeping victim, who subsequently captures and condemns Elvira. She escapes in time to contribute to his overthrow and death in battle. Anne so forcefully presented the penitent and fearless woman that a local critic asserted, "They must be devoid of sensibility, who could listen to her tale, unmoved." Although she had often portrayed equally violent characters driven to murder or self-destruction (Horatia,

---

[54] Dunlap, *History of the American Theatre*, II, 148.
[55] *Port Folio*, February 14, 1801, p. 52.
[56] Philadelphia *Gazette*, October 22, 1800.
[57] Elvira is another role originated by Mrs. Siddons, who was termed a wonder by her brother for creating a "heroine of a soldier's *trull*." Boaden, *Memoirs of John Philip Kemble*, II, 239.

Calista, Euphrasia, Palmira, Zara), some members of her audience preferred her as, and believed her better suited to, the melodrama's gentler character, Cora, the loving wife of Rolla who undergoes the torment of her husband's capture and the kidnapping of her child. One playgoer expressed his disapproval of the casting in the newspaper: "I am sorry to see in your paper . . . a Criticism on the Actors respecting the performance of Pizarro— the Person who did it is certainly no judge of his subject—as much as I admire Mrs. Merry; she was undoubtedly not in Character in Evira [sic]—in Cora she would have been *herself*."[58] But throughout the season the play continued to draw audiences, as did Anne, who sustained the role of Elvira "with the utmost energy and dignity."[59]

Another "very pleasing" portrayal which won accolades was that of Ophelia, whose mad scene earned special notice: "The fantastic appearance of her dress, the simplicity of her look, and the innocently wild manner in which she converses, must interest every beholder in the performance of so *great an actress*." Later in the season Anne gave the same characterization "that interest which her unrivalled excellence impresses upon every part, calculated to awaken the feelings. Her 'snatches of old tunes' were 'chaunted' with the most exquisite and touching simplicity." As Desdemona, she also merited "unqualified praise," and in her performance of the role of Euphrasia, for which she had "acquired great, and deserved reputation," she "justified the public approbation." In a new role, Zorayda, in M. G. Lewis' new comedy *The East Indian*, "her powers were never more electrical." An attentive audience and repeated bursts of applause testified that the young actress revealed, with believability, the anguish and despair of Zorayda. As Belvidera, she again "excited approbation from all, and drew tears from many." And more tears were shed in a première production of *Edwy and Elgiva*, a play by a Philadelphian, Charles Jared Ingersoll. "Mrs. Merry personated the persecuted queen with wonted excellence, and sang with such

[58] Philadelphia, *Gazette of the United States*, October 24, 27, 1800.
[59] *Port Folio*, February 14, 1801, p. 52.

'pleasing sorcery' that many a bright eye, in the boxes, glistened with sensibility."[60]

Although the quality of Anne's performances remained on the same high level of excellence as in preceding years and the content of her repertoire remained about the same as the previous season, the number of her appearances decreased from approximately one hundred of the year before to about sixty in 1800–1801. The newspapers and Warren's "journal" reveal that her delicate health took an increasingly noticeable toll on her stamina and ability to perform. In December her illness "unavoidably postponed" the opening of Lewis' *The East Indian.* Later in the season sickness prevented her from performing the roles of Mrs. Ford in *Merry Wives of Windsor,* Marcia in *Cato,* and Beatrice in *Much Ado About Nothing.*[61] During the Baltimore run her "sudden indisposition" postponed a performance of *Lovers' Vows* and cancelled *Castle Spectre.*[62] She was also ill during most of the benefit week but appeared again the closing night of the Baltimore spring season. Yet the siege of illness had taken its toll, forcing her to ask William Dunlap for a release from a commitment made in March for a brief summer engagement at the Park Theatre, New York. Dunlap received the request, written from Baltimore, on June 10, 1801.

> TO WM. DUNLAP, ESQ.
>
> Sir—To the last moment have I delayed writing, expecting that every hour would bring me a return of health; but heavy is this short task of telling you the opinion of my physicians, that my recovery is far distant; the complaint is in my breast, and is severe indeed; it has prevented my performing for many nights past, and I have given up the idea of being able to appear again this season.

60 Philadelphia, *Gazette of the United States,* October 27, 1800; *Port Folio,* February 28, 1801, p. 69, March 28, 1801, p. 102; Philadelphia, *Gazette of the United States,* December 23, 1800; *Port Folio,* March 28, 1801, p. 103, April 18, 1800, p. 127.
61 Philadelphia, *Gazette of the United States,* December 24, 1800; Warren, Journals, March 25, 27, 30, 1801.
62 Baltimore *American and Commercial Daily Advertiser,* April 25, 1801 hereinafter cited as Baltimore *American;* Warren, Journals, May 25, 1801.

I enclose a letter from Doctor Crawford, as my own feelings tell me his judgment is not erroneous; rash indeed would be the attempt of fulfilling my engagement with you this summer. Sincerely regretting the disappointment to myself and the inconvenience it may be to you, I remain, &c. &c.

A. MERRY [63]

Included with the letter was a note from her physician confirming her statement but giving little insight into the specific nature of her illness. When Dunlap replied that he had borrowed money in the belief that her performances would enable him to repay it and urged her to make at least two appearances for him and one for herself, she agreed to attempt the engagement. It is ironic perhaps, that Mrs. Merry, beset by ill health, was pulled so reluctantly into an engagement which gave her the distinction of being the first actor in America "brought forward as (what is now called) a star." And at that time, too, Warren was sufficiently impressed by the designation to note in his journal, "Mrs. Merry is acting as a Star in New York." [64] Her salary, commensurate with the title, paid her a hundred dollars a week plus a clear benefit, in contrast to thirty dollars per week offered to Cooper at the same engagement. [65]

For her first performance at the Park Theatre on July 1, she portrayed Belvidera, supported by John Hodgkinson as Jaffier and Cooper as Pierre. The remainder of her engagement included five of her most famous roles: Juliet, Calista, Beatrice, Monimia, and Horatia. Whether her precarious health affected the quality of her acting is difficult to determine. Dunlap states that in the performance of *The Fair Penitent*, Cooper's "unexpected excellence" as Lothario was "more vivid in our remembrance than any other portion of this perfect exhibition." Yet one account claiming that Mrs. Merry was "one uniform tissue of excellence" supports Durang's opinion that "she was a prodigious favorite at New

---

[63] Dunlap, *History of the American Theatre*, II, 150.
[64] *Ibid.*, 149; Warren, Journals, June 14, 1801.
[65] Dunlap, *History of the American Theatre*, II, 148.

York."[66] The New York critic attributed much of her success to her possession of the two great properties of a good speaker, voice and gesture. He judged that

> no one perhaps has a more perfect delivery, she seems to give every word its due emphasis, and every syllable its proper accent; her pauses are admirable, particularly her emphatic ones, and those too which make the divisions of sense; this last is never interrupted by a mismanagement of her breath. In her tones or the modulation of her voice she is equally unexceptionable, varying the sound to the sentiment she gives it that peculiar force and grace which the author designed. In action she is the child of nature, a most graceful motion of the hand, accompanied with a dignified attitude of the body, and one might tell her sentiments by the emotions of her countenance.[67]

Unfortunately, the engagement not only concluded unhappily with "a renewal of the great actress's indisposition" but with unpleasantness which she referred to in future years "with deepest regret."[68] Dunlap's account of the affair testifies to his high assessment of Anne as an "uncommonly fine woman" and dramatically illustrates her high box-office value.[69] The basic difficulty seems to have been the jealousy of actor John Hodgkinson, who together with his wife, was a member of the Park Theatre company. No doubt Dunlap correctly evaluated Hodgkinson's reaction to the importation of the eminent actress: "That Mrs. Merry should be brought to New York as the sun of drama, around which the great and little planets and their satellites were to revolve, was a sore mortification to one who could allow of no merit out of the precincts of his own family." At the same time Hodgkinson, recognizing that the "brilliancy of the lady's talent received the particular applause, attention, and patronage of the New York audience," wanted her to play for his benefit. But be-

[66] *Ibid.*, 151; Durang, "The Philadelphia Stage," Chap. XXXIV, December 24, 1854.
[67] New York *Commercial Advertiser*, July 9, 1801.
[68] Dunlap, *History of the American Theatre*, II, 151–52; Durang, "The Philadelphia Stage," Chap. XXXIV, December 24, 1854.
[69] Dunlap, *History of the American Theatre*, II, 157.

cause of her health she announced that she could not perform beyond her own benefit performance of *The Orphan* on Friday, July 10. When both Cooper and Hodgkinson subsequently asked her to remain for their respective nights, the actress answered "that if she could play, it would be for the manager."[70] The Monday following her benefit had been designated as Hodgkinson's night but he asked that it be postponed until Wednesday, an inconvenience to the management. After discussing and discarding several alternate proposals, Cooper volunteered to substitute Monday for his own benefit, provided that Anne would play for him. She agreed, with the understanding that Cooper would play for her benefit in Philadelphia; and, "as she had said she would only stay, if she stayed at all, for the manager's benefit, she insisted that half of the profits of the night should be his."[71] This news infuriated Hodgkinson, who asked her again to stay for his night also. When she declined and Hodgkinson implied that she wanted to be offered money, Mrs. Merry "expressed her disgust at his indelicacy" to Dunlap and stood firm on her refusal to play.[72] Hodgkinson retaliated by complaining to the public in his benefit play bills and in newspaper advertisements that he and his wife had been assured "the services of Mrs. Merry at their benefit, but that she had absolutely declined playing for them." In refuting the actor, Anne sought the help of William Coleman, who was to become editor of the *Evening Post* but who acted as her spokesman in the pages of the *Commercial Advertiser* over the signature of "Amicus." The heated exchange between Hodgkinson and Coleman almost led to "an appeal to the pistol," but tempers eventually cooled and Mrs. Merry returned to Philadel-

[70] *Ibid.*, 149; Durang, "The Philadelphia Stage," Chap. XXXIV, December 24, 1854; Dunlap, *History of the American Theatre*, II, 152.
[71] *Ibid.*, 155–56. Mrs. Merry seems to have been most concerned about not fulfilling her original agreement with Dunlap, who reported: "It is due to Mrs. Merry to state that, on the whole receipts of her benefit being presented to her, she would not receive the money, as her health had not permitted her to fulfill her original engagement; and with great difficulty she could be prevailed upon to accept, in addition to her salary, 750 of the 884 dollars received."
[72] *Ibid.*

phia without performing for Hodgkinson.[73] Her feelings of re-
proach toward the actor lingered, however, and are expressed in
a letter to Dunlap:

> —I own to you that I have been severely mortified to see my name
> so frequently before the public, in the New-York prints, and that
> attached to the name of a man whose conduct I despised, even
> before he had the opportunity of insulting me.
> This is the second public attack of Mr. Hodgkinson within a
> short space of time—the subjects females. Surely the people of
> your city must think of him as he deserves, and feel that all his
> assertions are indelicate, inhuman, and unmanly.
> On my return from the theatre, the last evening of my per-
> formance, I told Mr. Coleman that if he should observe any fur-
> ther insult from Mr. H. in the bills or papers, I must feel it as an
> obligation, as he was acquainted with all the circumstances, if he
> would answer for me; and not suffer Mr. H. to make an impres-
> sion on the public mind entirely in his own favour. I do feel my-
> self greatly obliged by Mr. Coleman, and only regret the *early* in-
> sertion of the first number of Amicus—all I wished was to stand
> on the defensive. I own myself a coward when armed against such
> a man, so unprincipled as Mr. H.[74]

Regardless of its transient character, the episode with Hodgkinson was an unpleasant conclusion to a year already compli-
cated by the distress of ill health. Yet, as Mrs. Merry began the
last year of her second three-year engagement with Wignell, she
probably was not regretting her decision to remain in the United
States. She hardly could have doubted that she had retained her
unrivaled position as the finest actress in America. But, at the
same time, this position, crowning her achievement as an artist
and insuring her own financial security, was a handicap to her
health. She appears to have been unable to withstand the American provincial theatre system, which required players to present
ever-changing bills in several distant cities. These demands were
especially exhausting for leading performers, who had to retain
not only a great number of characters in their repertoire but also

[73] *Ibid.*, II, 156, 157.
[74] *Ibid.*, 158–59.

had to carry the greatest burden in performance. As a result of her inability to sustain such a performance pattern, she could not complete her first starring engagement. If ill health appears to be an unfortunate aspect of the season of 1800–1801, it was undoubtedly something more: a prophetic harbinger that the American stage would lose, all too soon, its "brightest ornament."

V

Mrs. Merry Becomes Mrs. Wignell, Actress and Manager

1801-1805

Anne's return to Philadelphia probably was not accompanied by a return to the stage that summer. Most likely she took advantage of the remaining summer months to rest and recover her health. At the same time, a detachment of fellow actors from the Wignell and Reinagle company performed at the old colonial Southwark Theatre while workers remodeled the Chestnut Street theatre. Whatever course she followed to recuperate, on October 14, she was on hand for "repeated applause" in the opening production, as Miss Dorillon in *Wives as They Were and Maids as They Are*. In welcoming the Philadelphians to the newly decorated theatre, Wignell and Reinagle advertised that the smoking of "segars, . . . a practice so pregnant with danger, and so utterly repugnant to decorum," would not be permitted in the future. They also requested the "co-operation of the Public in abolishing the custom of giving away or disposing Checks at the doors of the Theatre"; for it tended to "encourage a crowd of idle boys and other disorderly persons about the Avenues of the Theatre, to the great annoyance of the audience by the clamourous importunity—and to the corruption of their own morals, by loitering away whole evenings at the doors."[1]

Just as the interior of the theatre was refurbished, so the company was also reinforced. Unhappily neither the ill-fated Fullerton, who committed suicide February 4, 1802, nor the newcomer, Jones, could compensate for the absence of Thomas Cooper, who had returned to the Park. Deprived of a leading tragedian to per-

[1] Philadelphia, *Gazette of the United States*, October 18, 1801.

form with Mrs. Merry, Wignell offered Philadelphia the next best thing: a second leading tragic actress. After an absence of five years Mrs. Whitlock, as well as her husband, was engaged not only to relieve Mrs. Merry's heavy schedule but also to feature rival talents. Since the two actresses had not encountered each other since the summer of 1797 in New York, when Anne won recognition as the superior actress, the "rival efforts" of the two actresses "excited much curiosity."[2]

A large audience (but a box office of almost a hundred dollars less than Mrs. Merry's first night) greeted Mrs. Whitlock's first appearance as Elwina in Hannah More's *Percy*.[3] An even larger crowd eagerly gathered on November 6 to witness the "great talents of Mrs. Merry and Mrs. Whitlock . . . united" for the first time in *Jane Shore*. Almost as an additional attraction, the actresses portrayed characters "different from what might have been expected, from a superficial calculation of their respective powers." Mrs. Merry's "magic sweetness" of tone seemed ideally suited to the "forlorn situation of the deserted Shore; while Mrs. Whitlock's energy would give full effect to the jealous ravings of the proud Alicia. But, by the opposite arrangement, the play was more perfectly performed."[4] No doubt the occasion reminded Anne of a similar situation years before at Covent Garden, when she enacted the role of Alicia to Mrs. Pope's portrayal of Jane Shore. At that time a Covent Garden critic asserted that the younger actress had been pushed into a character beyond her ability, because the "part of Alicia requires the well-matured genius of the first actress of the Stage."[5] Now, almost fifteen years later, a Philadelphia critic wrote: "Those who have witnessed Mrs. Merry in *Pizarro*, or her inimitable performance of the character now in question [Alicia], will readily admit, that her energy is adequate to the most difficult expression of passion." As if elaboration might do her injustice, the critic simply asserted,

---

[2] Wood, *Personal Recollections*, 83.
[3] *Ibid.*, Wood incorrectly identifies the character as Elvira.
[4] *Port Folio*, November 14, 1801, p. 364.
[5] See chapter 2, p. 21 above.

"Her performance left us nothing to desire." In contrast, he gave more detailed criticism of Mrs. Whitlock, pointing out that in general she was often too vehement, that she sometimes was artificial, and that in the expression of passion she occasionally distorted her features. However, in her portrayal of Jane Shore he thought: "These imperfections were very rarely observable. . . . The burst of mingled surprise and horror, upon meeting with her husband, was electrical, and her death awakened the sympathy, and excited the applause of the audience."[6]

Excitement in the pit heightened the interest of the evening. Just as Alexander Cain "was pronouncing over the [Jane's] body, the moral of the play, . . . Some person in one of the front boxes, suddenly sprung from his seat, exclaiming the gallery was falling." An additional cry of Fire caused general panic. "A crowd of people from the front boxes" rushed "into the pit—several ladies . . . upon the stage . . ." before they learned it was a false alarm and the audience settled down to witness the popular after-piece *Blue Beard*.[7]

The box-office receipts of $920 probably encouraged Wignell to schedule the combined talents of the two actresses only five nights later with Anne's first American appearance in *The Mourning Bride*. As the gentle, anguished Almeria, she again received Oliver Oldschool's unqualified praise: ". . . it was fully equal to any specimen of her wonderful talents, that the public has yet witnessed. It was a perfect performance." Mrs. Whitlock, portraying the role of rejected and incensed Zara, also earned "the highest praise, with one exception only. It appeared . . . that, in the scene with Osmyn, where her jealousy burst forth, her agitations were rather those of the jealous wife, than of the haughty Zara."[8]

"To the lovers of the higher species of drama," Wignell offered in December another rich treat when the actresses performed together in the *Earl of Essex*. Postponed from December 4 until

6 *Port Folio*, November 14, 1801, p. 364–65.
7 *Ibid.*, 365.
8 *Ibid.*, 366.

December 9 because of Mrs. Merry's illness, the production "attracted a numerous and fashionable auditory." "Well supported" throughout, it received, "unmixed approbation." Mrs. Whitlock portrayed the English queen "with characteristic dignity," representing her "haughty port" and "impetuous passions" with "appropriate energy." Mrs. Merry, appearing as the distraught secret wife of Essex, "displayed her usual resistless sway over the passions of the spectators."[9] A new production, *Joanna of Montfaucon*, adapted by Richard Cumberland from the German of Kotzebue, provided another opportunity to compare the two actresses. "Cast with the whole strength of the house," the drama was "well acted" by all, including the rival performers, who sustained their parts "with their wonted perfection."[10]

If Philadelphians anticipated a bitter rivalry they must have been disappointed. Anne's dislike for professional unpleasantness and distasteful publicity is evident from her letter to Dunlap concerning the Hodgkinson controversy. Moreover no evidence suggests that an open personal competition existed between the women. Records do make clear that they extended professional courtesies to one another. During Mrs. Merry's lengthy illness, which prevented her from performing between December 30, 1801, and February 3, 1802, Mrs. Whitlock carried the leading roles and performed the part of Fanny for her in *The Clandestine Marriage*.[11] For Anne's benefit performance on March 10 of *Pizarro*, which attracted a "highly fashionable and splendid" audience, Mrs. Whitlock "ably supported" the role of Elvira instead of Mrs. Merry, who, noted the critic, performed "the more humble, though we think not less interesting, part of Cora."[12] The assignment of roles for *Pizarro* rather typifies the castings for the two women throughout the year; Mrs. Whitlock tended toward the strong, forceful heroines (Zara, Millwood,

[9] *Ibid.*, December 12, 1801, p. 398.
[10] *Ibid.*, February 13, 1802, p. 43.
[11] Warren, Journals, January 6, 1802.
[12] *Port Folio*, March 27, 1802, pp. 89–90.

Elizabeth, and Lady Macbeth) while Mrs. Merry most often played the more loving, passionate ones (Juliet, Cora, Ophelia, and the Countess of Rutland).

In addition to appearing together, each actress maintained a busy individual schedule. Mrs. Merry acted mainly in stock pieces and learned only five new roles during the entire year. But whether she performed with Mrs. Whitlock in national premières or in revivals, she received what had become customary acclaim. Although her excellence as Euphrasia had been long established, the *Port Folio* critic considered it a " 'bounden duty' to notice the wonderful excellence of Mrs. Merry, in that character . . . . In the last act in particular, where she rescued her father, by the death of the tyrant, she almost excelled herself, and the admiration of the audience was expressed, by repeated bursts of well merited applause." A week later, on November 27, her portrayal of the role of Sigismunda "was, as usual, a finished specimen of the scenic art." The repetition of phrases of tribute became an acknowledged problem for the reviewer, who complained: "Unless we could infinitely vary the language of praise, we must be reduced to tiresome repetition, in our account of this lady's performances. We have, therefore, sometimes entertained the idea, an idea soothing to our 'lettered indolence,' that we would omit to speak of her, till she gave us some reason to find fault with her."[13] In spite of this difficulty, the critic continued to praise Anne for her artistry in investing a characterization with more interest than the script suggests. He noted this achievement when she portrayed Bertha in *Point of Honour* and, again, when she appeared as Miss Courtney in *The Dramatist*, he found that "although the part seems beneath her powers, she imparted to it interest and importance."[14]

Concerning Mrs. Whitlock's acting, Oldschool reported that her characterization of Lady Randolph in *Douglas* brought expressions of "unmixed gratification, and . . . unqualified applause." As Mrs. Oakley in *The Jealous Wife*, he said that she gave such a

13 *Ibid.*, December 5, 1801, p. 390.
14 *Ibid.*, February 27, 1802, p. 57; March 27, 1802, p. 90.

"perfect delineation of female jealousy and rage" that she was favorably compared with her sister Mrs. Siddons: "In *the tempest of passion*, the energetic utterance, and the expressive features of this lady, have a wonderful effect upon the scrutinizing spectator, and perpetually remind him of the name of *Siddons*." Some reviewers, however, suggest that not all of her performances could merit the Merry label of "finished excellence." After Mrs. Whitlock appeared as Portia in *The Merchant of Venice*, the critic thought it "but just to speak with much complacency," and her appearance as Elvina in *Percy* drew qualified approval:

> Her conception of many parts of the
> character was excellent, but she
> occasionally sinned against the
> precept of Lloyd.
>   "The word and action should conjointly
> suit,
>   But *acting words* is labour too minute,"
> We would point out the following line, in
> particular, as an instance in which this
> rule was violated.
>   "I sigh'd, I struggled, fainted, and
> complied."[15]

Such comments suggest that although the appearance of the two women undoubtedly created considerable interest, rival followings, and, above all, high quality in performances, Mrs. Whitlock did not seriously threaten Mrs. Merry as the leading actress in the Chestnut Street company. Reviews of combined and separate performances praise both actresses, but, inevitably, qualifications attend the criticism of Mrs. Whitlock's performances. At the end of the season, when she and her husband once again withdrew from the Chestnut Street company, Anne could anticipate renewing her contract in the fall of 1802, eminently secure in her position as foremost actress on the American stage.

In spite of the popularity of the two actresses, the company suffered a box office slump in mid-season, and Wignell and Rei-

15 *Ibid.*, October 31, 1801, p. 350; December 5, 1801, p. 390; February 13, 1802, p. 42; December 26, 1801, p. 411; October 31, 1801, p. 350.

nagle suspended performances between February 18 and February 22 "for want of sufficient encouragement from the town."[16] Old-school first expressed concern over the "melancholy spectacle of a house nearly deserted," after he attended the new Kotzebue production *Joanna of Montfaucon* on February 5. He feared: "The frequent repetition of this circumstance, . . . will paralyze their future efforts. If the practice of collecting numerous and splendid parties upon the nights appropriated to theatrical per-formances, should continue; it is impossible but that the man-agers must sustain a heavy loss at the close of the season."[17]

An editorial in the *Gazette* suggests that the Quakers were in-directly encouraging the ruin of the managers, but chastisement from Oldschool may have had some effect upon theatre patrons; for when the theatre reopened with a production of *Point of Honour*, Oldschool "rejoiced at seeing the boxes respectably filled, notwithstanding the inclemency of the weather" ("storm—snow —wind—hail, the very worst day this winter").[18] In another per-formance of *Point of Honour* Anne shared billing with one of the most novel attractions of the year. On March 4, in addition to the comedy, the management offered "Shawnese and Delaware Chiefs" (who were "on tour of the U.S.") dancing "their country dances, particularly, *The Corn Piece, The Eagle Piece* and *The War Dance*." The dances were followed by an address by the principal chief. William Wood recalled that, "These dancers were . . . so terribly in earnest, that in their furor piece after piece of their scanty drapery became so unfixed and disarranged, as to occasion the flight of several ladies from the boxes."[19] Neverthe-less box-office receipts of $1,006 must have encouraged Wignell to chance further injury to delicate sensibilities because he sched-uled the Indian program again a few nights later. Unfortunately,

---

[16] Warren, Journals, February 16, 1802; Philadelphia, *Gazette of the United States*, February 16, 1802.
[17] *Port Folio*, February 13, 1802, p. 43.
[18] *Ibid.*, February 27, 1802, p. 57; Warren, Journals, February 22, 1802.
[19] Philadelphia, *Gazette of the United States*, March 4, 1802; Wood, *Personal Recollections*, 86.

appearing on a night preceding the beginning of the benefit season, the dancers brought box-office receipts of only $340.

As in previous years Mrs. Merry led off the benefit performances. However, this time her box-office total of $1,000.75 was less than that of two others; Bernard's night earned $1,260 (Mrs. Merry played on this occasion) and Francis' receipts brought $1,150.[20] Regrettably, for purposes of comparison, neither of the Whitlocks received a benefit. The significance of the benefit totals in matters of finance as well as prestige was sadly evident that year when Mrs. Oldmixon's night drew disappointing receipts of $520. By the end of the fourth act of the evening's comedy, the distressed actress had become so ill that she had to be "carried home . . . her illness occasioned chiefly by the House having fail'd—she expected a very great one.—" One other benefit performance that spring is noteworthy because as Ophelia (on Cain's night) Anne's performance caused one anonymous admirer, writing in the pages of the Philadelphia *Daily Advertiser*, to compare her once again to her old rival.

TO MRS. MERRY.

MADAM,

The enjoyment I derive from your exquisite performance of OPHELIA, on Friday evening, will not permit me to proceed on my tour, without leaving behind this testimony, however trifling, of my respect for your talents; and tho' unfortunately an entire stranger to you, allow me to add, that such tribute can only appear singular to those who have never witnessed your excellence in holding "as 'twere, the mirror up to nature."

I have but little hesitation in asserting that Mrs. Siddons, at the climax of her celebrity, could not have produced a greater effect on human feelings, than your most inimitable powers justly acquired you. For the truth of this remark, I appeal to those (and

---

[20] In addition to a performance of *The Distressed Mother*, Francis advertised an elaborate procession. His audience assumed that the participating figures would be live actors but playgoers were incensed to discover pasteboard cut-outs instead. Wood claimed that "from this time forward the announcement of Francis's name for a benefit, was the never failing pledge of an empty house." Wood, *Personal Recollections*, 88.

there were many present) who have seen you both on stage.

. . . .

So long, Madam, as nature remains true to her own character, you may securely calculate on the sensibility and applause of the part of your audience devoted to the tender charities of life at home as well as on the heart-felt admiration and gratitude of the

TRAVELER[21]

Concerning the effectiveness of the same performance, Oldschool remarked that Mrs. Merry "almost excelled her former excellence. Her 'snatches of old tune' were given 'in wringing tone so soothe,' that many an eye was moistened with sympathy."[22]

The benefits concluded with a brief visit from Thomas Cooper, who appeared again for Wignell's night, April 9, when the manager offered a new production, M. G. Lewis' *Adelmorn*. Playgoers enthusiastically endorsed his appearance, bringing in box-office totals of $1,069 for the presentation of *Adelmorn* and $1,067 for his second night's appearance in *Hamlet*. When the curtain fell "the audience call'd for another play—for Cooper to act in—."[23] On the following night Cooper played one of his favorite roles, Penruddock in *The Wheel of Fortune*. This performance was the last one before the Wignell and Reinagle actors departed for Baltimore to open their spring season, four days later on April 19.

On the same day, Mrs. Merry, instead of accompanying the Philadelphia troupe, opened a two-week engagement in New York, which Odell distinguished "as far as acting is concerned" the "highwater mark" of Dunlap's entire period of management.[24] The roles which she played during this time are as impressive as her supporting players and the receipts which the performances brought:

April 19   Juliet $1,000 Cooper as Romeo;
                                          Hallam as Mercutio

[21] Warren, Journals, March 20, 1802; Philadelphia *Daily Advertiser*, March 29, 1802.
[22] *Port Folio*, April 17, 1802, p. 107.
[23] Warren, Journals, April 14, 1802.
[24] Odell, *Annals of the New York Stage*, II, 137.

April 22 [21]	Calista	676	Cooper as Lothario; Hodgkinson as Horatio
April 24 [23]	Belvidera	624	Cooper as Pierre; Hodgkinson as Jaffier
April 26	Isabella	760	Cooper as Biron; Hodgkinson as Villeroy
April 28	Lady Teazle	750	Hallam as Sir Peter; Hodgkinson as Charles
April 30	[Alicia]	800	Mrs. Hodgkinson as Jane Shore; Cooper as Hastings
May 3	Monimia	900	Cooper as Chamont; Hodgkinson as Castalio[25]

"Thespis," critic of the newly established New York *Evening Post*, has left not only glowing tributes to the lady's artistry but also helpful descriptions of her acting. At an early hour on the night opening her engagement, "a more brilliant assemblage than was ever known on a holiday night" crowded the house and filled boxes with "ladies of first fashion."[26] When the visiting star made her first entrance as Juliet, "loud and reiterated welcome was heard in every part of the house. This tumultuous expression of their delight gave place, at the first word she uttered, to the more characteristic manner of our audience.—*Hush! she speaks!* seemed to be the common sensation." "Thespis" commented on "the magic sweetness" of Anne's voice as Juliet; and in her performance of Calista he praised "her expressive manner of filling up pauses and listening to the conversation of others," a characteristic which also distinguished her great English model and rival Mrs. Siddons.[27] The critic particularly noted that in the letter scene with Horatio, "the surprise, apprehension and varied emotions of conscious guilt . . . are elegantly marked during her silence as by the most expressive language." In addition to its sweetness, her voice must have richly revealed shades of emotion, for

[25] Dunlap, *History of the American Theatre*, II, 163.
[26] New York *Evening Post*, April 20, 1802.
[27] *Ibid.*, April 23, 1802.

"Thespis" claimed that she conveyed "in the compass of a single sentence, the grief, shame and despair of the *lost* Calista. These faculties, aided by a powerful and energetic delivery when the circumstances of the scene call for strong exertion, enable her to exhibit the ever varying and almost evanescent shades of passion with a truth and accuracy, that delights while it astonishes her audience."

As Belvidera, Anne further demonstrated that her face, like that of Mrs. Siddons, was equally rich in expression.

> In her first interview with *Jaffier*, her expressive listening . . . was strikingly observable. Her eager countenance, seemed to anticipate his very thoughts . . . every feature of her face bespeaks the emotions of her soul, and before her tongue has given utterance to the sentiment, she has already told him all *her love*.
>
> The dullest observer could not fail to remark the surprise, astonishment and fearful apprehension pourtrayed in her looks and gesture, when *Jaffier* delivered her over to the conspirators as the hostage of his fidelity . . . she seems to doubt her own senses, and vainly looks round, in wild amazement, for the solution.[28]

The same review described the eloquence of the combination of the "thrilling tones of her voice" and the expressive use of her body when "in pronouncing the last words, she stretched forth her arm and seemed to rise from the earth with the proud consciousness of all the greatness of soul that distinguished the wife of Brutus." Poor health beset her once again during the second week of the engagement and Anne's performance as Lady Teazle suffered. Although "her appearance was engaging; her performance sprightly, elegant, and graceful . . . it wanted vivacity"; and in addition, she needed help from the prompter. Nevertheless, she completed her second starring engagement, concluding with two of her most notable roles, Alicia and Monimia. Her benefit receipts of $900 combined with her other profits for a total of "better than $1,100" for the brief and highly successful engagement.[29]

---

[28] *Ibid.*, April 26, 1802.
[29] *Ibid.*, April 30, 1802; Warren, Journals, May 10, 1802.

One week later Mrs. Merry rejoined the Chestnut Street company in Baltimore. Between May 10 and June 11 she appeared approximately fourteen times in thirteen different plays. During the last week her ill health once again forced the managers to change the announced bill from *Pizarro* to *Deaf and Dumb*.[30] With her health obviously a continuing problem, the actress probably decided to rest for the entire summer after the Baltimore season ended on June 11. Records do not reveal her exact whereabouts but Warren indicates that a recurrence of yellow fever emptied Philadelphia of playgoers as well as performers.[31] Like them she may have gone to New Jersey and the neighboring villages. Forced to give up an attempt at summer theatricals at the Southwark, William Warren remained in the deserted city because his wife was expecting their first child. However, in September he collected the scattered flock of actors for a two-week engagement in Annapolis. Warren's list of the company names eight actors, five actresses, a tailor, a property man, a painter, and a call boy, but does not mention Mrs. Merry. Most likely she did not perform again until the opening of the Baltimore fall season on November 8.

When she resumed her acting in the fall, Anne performed under a renewed contract with Thomas Wignell.[32] She did not seem to hesitate at this time to remain with the Chestnut Street group. Undoubtedly the widow also decided to commit her private as well as her professional life to Wignell's care; but wedding plans did not disrupt the regular fall schedule. Out of the seventeen performances in Baltimore between November 8 and December 4, 1802, Wignell scheduled eight plays in which Mrs. Merry normally carried leading roles.[33] Upon returning to Philadelphia she performed in six plays before the New Year. In the week between Christmas and New Year, she helped to provide Philadelphians with a holiday treat by appearing with Cooper

---

[30] *Ibid.*, June 7, 1802.
[31] *Ibid.*, September 9–October 28, 1802.
[32] Durang, "The Philadelphia Stage," Chap. XXXVI, January 7, 1855.
[33] Warren, Journals.

during his brief four-night engagement. Together they performed in *Hamlet, Richard III,* and *Venice Preserv'd.*[34] On December 31 the latter performance was their last one together prior to Cooper's departure for Europe and Anne's marriage to Wignell. In the final one Cooper played Macbeth with Mrs. Barrett, a newcomer engaged as a replacement for Mrs. Whitlock as Lady Macbeth. On the same day, January 1, 1803, the Reverend Mr. Abercrombie married Mrs. Merry to Thomas Wignell in a ceremony "at the house N. E. corner of South Street and Sansom Row," probably Wignell's residence.[35]

The marriage seems to have been the inevitable result of their mutual trust and close professional relationship and, possibly, a change in values for the actress. Evidence indicates a wide difference between the personalities of Mrs. Merry's first and second husbands. From descriptions by those who worked under his management, Wignell emerges as an opposite of the dashing, fun-loving, and quixotic Merry. At age thirty-three and in her circumstances, the young widow may have admired and needed the steadfastness which Wignell possessed. "The four corner-stones which supported the basis of Mr. Wignell's character were, Candour, Truth, Integrity, and Honour. . . . the whole with all its beauty, had its strength: it supported vexation, disappointment, treachery, and adversity—a heavy weight: . . . and never did one cornerstone give way," wrote James Fennell. In a less formal description, Fennell suggests Wignell as one who earned the affection of his associates: "He had always that portion of wit and anecdote at command, which his part in the promotion of pleasures of society required; but never suffered either to be intrusive. He was witty without vanity, and didactic without pride. His guests were pleased on entering his house, and left it highly gratified; for good humour gave the inspiring welcome, and good humour gave the necessary

---

[34] Philadelphia, *Gazette of the United States,* December 27–December 31, 1802. The writer gratefully acknowledges the research assistance of Patricia Harris Burgin, who obtained data used in this study from Philadelphia newspapers published between November, 1802, and May, 1808.

[35] *Ibid.,* January 3, 1803; Warren, Journals, January 1, 1803.

adieu."[36] William Wood, who had begun his theatrical apprenticeship under Wignell's guidance, called him "an invaluable
friend and father." Charles Durang remembered that "his private
character and gentlemanly deportment ever inspired the esteem
and respect of all his friends and acquaintances. We have often
heard our valued friends, Mr. William Francis and Mr. Blissett
speak in the most exalted terms of the commendation of Thomas
Wignell, eulogizing his stern integrity, urbanity and correct principles—the model of the man and gentleman." Durang described
him: "He was not tall, was rather thick set, wearing his hat a little
on one side, a small stick in his hand, and spencer over his coat."[37]
Durang's father John, who knew Wignell as a fellow member of
the Old American Company and also as an employer in the Chestnut Street company, acknowledged him as a "good friend," and
"a worthy gentleman and man of honour."[38] From testimonial
and description, Wignell appears to have been a fitting partner
for the actress whose private conduct from her earliest professional
years was such "as would grace a woman of superior rank."[39] After
she had been in America only two years, one writer asserted that
she was "not less esteemed for her public talents than for the
strict propriety of her conduct in private life, and she stands a
bright and confessed exception, to that too general prejudice entertained concerning the private virtues of dramatic performers."
William Dunlap looked upon her as a "very superior" and "uncommonly fine" woman. Durang admired her as the "very personification of courtesy."[40] Except for Hodgkinson's accusations
during the unpleasant New York engagement in 1801, few testi-
monials survive which detract from her character. If successful

[36] Fennell, An Apology . . . for James Fennell, 366, 367.
[37] Wood, Personal Recollections, 92; Durang, "The Philadelphia Stage," Chap.
XXXVI, January 7, 1855.
[38] Durang, The Memoir of John Durang, 105, 106.
[39] London Daily Universal Register, December 13, 1786.
[40] Thomas Condie, "Biographical Anecdotes of Mrs. Merry of the Theatre, Philadelphia," Philadelphia Monthly Magazine . . . , I (April, 1798), 187; Dunlap,
History of the American Theatre, II, 149, 157; Durang, "The Philadelphia Stage,"
Chap. XXXI, December 3, 1854.

unions are built on similarity of values, character traits, and interests, it appears that the newly married couple had every reason to anticipate a happy marriage.

The actress appeared for the first time as Mrs. Wignell on January 12, 1803, in the role of Rosamunda in a new offering, Dunlap's version of *Abaellino, the Great Bandit* from the German of Johan Zschokke. "A very fashionable and numerous audience" congratulated her "in a most ardent and friendly manner." She responded to this "expression of public regard with respectful sensibility" and with a performance that "was excessively engaging in the representation of the innocence & ardor of female passion. She was an interesting compound of vivacity, love, fear and hope." Durang often saw her appear in this play afterwards and could "never forget the simplicity and truth with which she invested it."[41] Although scheduled next to appear in *The Castle Spectre* on Saturday, January 15, 1803, her sudden indisposition made it necessary for her husband to substitute Mrs. Barrett at the last minute. One theatregoer, "F," was so indignant over the replacement that he accused the management of deliberately withholding the announcement until after patrons had entered the theatre in order not to discourage attendance. This accusation stimulated a series of exchanges in the newspaper.[42] Interpreting the remarks as unjust attacks on his wife, Wignell published an indignant reply which included a letter from Dr. Benjamin Rush testifying that he had forbidden the actress to perform on the day in question. In a lengthy letter "F" countered that his "communication" in no way was meant to "injure or offend a lady who has always been the object of our admiration and the theme of our praise." Rather, he maintained that he was accusing the management of deliberately deceiving the audience. Finally, to settle the affair, William Warren published Wignell's order for the substitution written at a late hour on Saturday the day of the performance:

[41] Philadelphia *Gazette*, January 13, 1803; Durang, "The Philadelphia Stage," Chap. XXXVI, January 7, 1855.
[42] Philadelphia *Gazette*, January 17, 22, 24, 27, 28, 1803.

DEAR WARREN,

   Read the enclosed and send it to Mrs. B. and have the good-ness to call for her answer—if she cannot play the part, Deaf and Dumb, or Speed the Plough must be the substitute. I am waiting to see Mrs. W. bled or I would have come down myself.

   You will find me at home,

Your's &c.   T. W.

The incident seems to have had no lasting effect, but it testifies to the prominent role Mrs. Wignell continued to play in the wel-fare of the company and the degree to which the actors were held responsible to their audience.

   During February, Philadelphians were offered the unexpected special attraction of the talents of James Fennell and John Hodgkinson, whose few appearances provided Mrs. Wignell an opportunity to perform in *Othello* and *Venice Preserv'd*. Box-office receipts indicate that audiences enthusiastically supported the visiting actors, but equal enthusiasm may not have prevailed backstage. On the night of Fennell's appearance as Othello, War-ren complained in his journal: "The New York Theatre being shut for two weeks, Hodgkinson and Fennell came in a manner to force an Engagement by Raising a tumult in the City—Coop-er's success has been the cause—why these Lads annoy us and their Desire to Raise the wind."[43] As early as January 21 the Philadel-phia *Gazette and Public Advertiser* had published the rumor that Hodgkinson "with a detachment of the New-York company" planned to perform in the Old Theatre for a short time. If such were actually the case, Wignell undoubtedly sought to employ the actors as visiting performers rather than suffer such serious competition. However Wignell regarded the visit from the New York players, he nevertheless entertained them with a dinner party Thursday, February 10.[44] That same morning he had been bled with a spring lancet. On Saturday, as an additional courtesy he invited Fennell to share his private box with him for Hodgkin-son's performance as Macbeth. But during the performance, Wig-

---

[43] Warren, Journals, February 12, 1803.
[44] *Ibid.*, February 14, 1803.

nell's infected arm became so painful that he was forced to excuse himself from Fennell's company.[45] By Sunday, February 13, the infection had increased to such a perilous degree that it threatened his life, which the combined efforts of Doctors Wistar, Park, and Rush could not save.[46] On February 21, just seven weeks after his marriage, Wignell died.

On the following day the funeral gave just tribute to a man who had done more in his lifetime than any other individual to improve the quality of American theatre. "His funeral ceremonies were most imposing. His body was followed to St. Peter's [Episcopal] Church . . . where he was buried by a cortège of the most respectable citizens of Philadelphia. The wealthy sent their private carriages, and paid other demonstrations of respect. Early in the afternoon the church was filled [by] our citizens of all classes."[47]

On the day after the funeral the newspaper carried a significant and melancholy announcement which marked the beginning of a new era for the Chestnut Street theatre as well as a new phase in the theatrical career of Mrs. Wignell. The advertisement stated that the theatre would continue to operate under the direction of Mrs. Wignell and Reinagle, "with the assistance of Messrs. Warren and Wood, as acting managers." Warren "principally attended to the acting management," (a position assumed in the fall of 1799 at an increase in salary of five dollars a week), whereas Wood acted as "*quasi* stage manager."[48] Undoubtedly the new manageress depended almost entirely on these men to operate the theatre during her bereavement, when she also withdrew from performing. Following the death of her husband, she did not rejoin the company until April 18, after it had moved to Baltimore for the spring season.[49] During that engagement she probably par-

[45] Fennell, *An Apology for . . . James Fennell*, 365–66.
[46] Warren, Journals, February 14, 1803.
[47] Durang, "The Philadelphia Stage," Chap. XXXVI, January 7, 1855.
[48] Philadelphia, *Gazette of the United States*, February 23, 1803; Warren, Journals, October 14, 1799; Durang, "The Philadelphia Stage," Chap. XXXVIII, January 21, 1855.
[49] Warren, Journals, April 18, 1803.

ticipated in about seventeen performances of fourteen different roles. Two new roles, Amelrosa, in M. G. Lewis' *Alfonso, King of Castile,* and Lilla, in Dunlap's adaptation of *The Voice of Nature,* proved to be popular attractions in Philadelphia the following winter.

The close of the Baltimore season was accompanied by a variety of activities within the company and a loss of some of the acting personnel, including such important performers as the Bernards and Mrs. Barrett. Wood made a recruiting excursion to England while Warren managed the rest of the company in Annapolis and Upper Marlboro between June 17 and September 29. (Warren and Reinagle had endeavored "to make arrangements for a Theatre in George Town" but "did not succeed to . . . [their] wishes.")[50] Anne did not participate in the summer engagement, withdrawing from performances until after the birth of her daughter Elizabeth in the fall of 1803.[51]

The spring of 1803 must have been another difficult period for the actress. She faced several choices: returning to England after the birth of her child, continuing with the Chestnut Street company as co-manager and leading actress, or remaining in the capacity of leading actress only. By May she had made a definite commitment. She and Reinagle leased the Chestnut Street theatre for four years at an estimated rental of $2,500 a year.[52] Dunlap preserved a letter telling of her final decision to remain with the Chestnut Street company:

---

[50] *Ibid.,* June 7, 1803.

[51] After her mother's death, Elizabeth remained with Warren (Mrs. Wignell's third husband) until she married Peter Benson (born in Philadelphia, November 28, 1795; a graduate, A.B. of the University of Pennsylvania in 1812, and A.M. in 1816) in a ceremony performed by the Reverend William White at St. Peter's Church where her father was buried. Undoubtedly the William White who officiated at her wedding also conducted her father's funeral services twenty years earlier. The Bensons moved to Cincinnati where he was cashier in the United States Branch Bank. Several children were born to the couple but their names and the names of their descendants are not known. See W. A. Newman Dorland, "The Second Troop Philadelphia City Cavalry," *Pennsylvania Magazine of History and Biography,* XLVI (1922), 270.

[52] Durang, "The Philadelphia Stage," Chap. XXXVI, January 7, 1855.

Baltimore, May 30th, 1803

W. Dunlap, Esq.

Dear Sir,—Before this time you must have seen by the papers that I have bound myself a slave for four years. Doubts and fears for the consequences of such an arduous undertaking prevented my answering your kind and friendly letter before. As I did not make up my mind to the task until the last moment, and as circumstances would have obliged me to remain in this country at least to the end of the next winter, it is more than probable I should have accepted your proposal, and be assured this is the only reason for my apparent neglect. Believe me, with all respect,

Your obedient and obliged friend,
Anne Wignell[53]

Her decision to assume the management of the company for a four-year period may have been influenced by a hope of obtaining the services of her brother. A brief newspaper item revealed: "Mr. Brunton, Mrs. Wignell's brother, is said, will shortly come to this country with a theatrical reinforcement." Another report from a London paper more than a year later indicated that he was still expected in Philadelphia as late as December, 1804: "Mr. Brunton sets off to America, to join his sister's Company, as soon as the Brighton season closes. He is a respectable Actor, and will take with him an unimpeachable character in private life."[54] Why Brunton did not fulfill his plans and come to the United States is unknown. Probably as a consequence of his not joining her, Mrs. Wignell eventually turned over her share of the management to Warren, and after Reinagle's death in 1809 the Chestnut Street theatre management was jointly assumed by Warren and Wood. In her letter to Dunlap, Anne suggests that she anticipated assuming full responsibilities as a manager of the theatre. Nevertheless the extent of her participation is difficult to determine. Undoubtedly she influenced the company policy considerably, as a brief item in Warren's journal suggests. On November 14, 1803, "Morris prevailed on Mrs. Wignell to let him make another effort." Although the circumstances surrounding this incident are

[53] Dunlap, *History of the American Theatre*, II, 192.
[54] Philadelphia *Gazette*, May 16, 1803; December 6, 1804.

not known, it is most likely only one of many which caused John Durang to comment after the management devolved upon Mrs. Wignell, "I was sorry to see her in the situation, harrass'd by some of the performers as she was."[55] Charles Durang amusingly describes another instance when, as a youth, he beheld her exert authority in matters of the wardrobe.

> Cain was extremely careless in his dressing, and even at times manifested a want of cleanliness. His "tights" . . . looked like a loose garment thrown on his person hap-hazard. On one special occasion, he was playing Romeo to the Juliet of . . . Mrs. Wignell. . . . At the fall of the curtain, at the end of the play, . . . amidst the most thundering applause . . . Mrs. Wignell arose, as we thought, obviously excited, and hastened to the green-room. . . . With the rude curiosity of a boy, we followed her to the green-room, for we did love and honor our managerial queen above all others. With evident feeling, she directed the master tailor, McCubbins, to be called to her; she also desired the presence of Mr. Cain, before he disrobed himself of his Romeo habiliments. After the two persons thus summoned appeared before her, she descanted in very strong terms upon the dress of Mr. Cain, rebuking both the actor and the costumer, for their violation of everything like propriety and suitableness in "her Romeo's" dress. . . . She concluded by ordering the master of the robes to make an entire new dress for Mr. Cain, and to be very particular hereafter, when he had a principal part to play with her, to see him suitably equipped at all points.[56]

During her reign as manager, Anne probably did not inaugurate any new policies and most likely attempted to maintain the company in much the same fashion as had her husband. Under her direction it continued the same seasonal schedules in Baltimore and Philadelphia, while independent summer engagements were undertaken by the actors wherever and whenever they could find the most suitable arrangements. Company replacements came from other American companies or as the result of special recruiting missions to England, such as that undertaken by Wood. Anne also probably encouraged Wood to conduct rehearsals "with

[55] John Durang, Memoir, 117–18.
[56] Durang, "The Philadelphia Stage," Chap. XXXI, December 3, 1854.

all the regularity and strict order of a night's performance." Durang has described the procedure in detail.

> The stage was set—that is, the flats were in their grooves agree-
> able to the requirement of the scene plot; the properties were
> ready for use, as called for by the property plot, before the
> rehearsal commenced. The time of rehearsals was as promptly
> attended to as the ringing up the curtain at night. The scene-
> shifters were at their respective stations to answer the prompter's
> whistle by changing the scenes. The property-man and the stage-
> clearers were at the proper entrances, with the tables and chairs,
> to place them in their appropriate situations, as the business of
> the scene required; so that all the details of the performances,
> bating the costumes, were *minutely*, . . . ceremoniously and de-
> corously, gone through with. No actor was allowed to cross the
> line mark of any entrance that was embraced in the scene then
> acting at night or at the rehearsal in the morning. The green-
> rooms were appropriated and properly furnished for the quiet
> and orderly assemblage of the company, to be called thence only
> morning and night, by the call-boy, for the duties of the stage.
> There was no restraint to go where they chose; but there was
> never any violation on good order behind the scenes in the day;
> the performers regarded their duties in the day as if the audience
> were assembled in front.[57]

Mrs. Wignell exerted influence off-stage as well as on, for Durang
testified that the greenroom "was a drawing room in every sense
of the word; where the presence of Mrs. Merry, Mrs. Whitlock,
Mrs. Melmoth, Mrs. Wood, and other ladies of cultivated intel-
lect and polished manners, were examples to the younger members of the profession, who felt a restraint and respect before
them."[58]

New duties as manager and mother as well as leading actress
left Anne little time for social life, yet Durang remembered her
as the "directress" and social matron.

> In the refined and polished circles of Philadelphia, Baltimore and
> Annapolis, Mrs. Merry was ever received with every consideration
> due to the character of a lady. . . . Wherever she appeared, either
> off or on the boards, a most profound respect from all classes

[57] *Ibid.*, Chap. XXX, October 26, 1854.
[58] *Ibid.*

seemed anxious to show itself in her honor. Her majesty of mien and dignified deportment were softened by the most winning blandishment of manners. The amiable characteristics of the kind gentlewoman were so openly and sweetly developed that her inferiors in business always approached her with cheerfulness, and would devote their every energy to her interests with untiring zeal. The literary circles of our cities felt the impress of her intellectual beauties.[59]

Durang also recalled Anne's impressive arrival at the theatre

in her chariot of simple but elegant structure, drawn by two very favorite sorrel horses, well matched, and of great beauty and docility. The coachman was a genteel white man, dressed in a kind of half livery—a gray surtout, buckskin breeches, and fair-top boots. The whole equipage was always admired for its extreme neatness and elegance. . . . With her, everything that her magic wand touched became a personification of chasteness. There was a charm about the old chariot and sorrel horses that spoke of fashion, of respectability, and of standing in society, which imparted dignity to the directress of the theatre, and, as a consequence of all these impressions, shed similar influences on the profession. When the chariot of this lady stood before the door of the theatre . . . of a morning waiting for her to finish her business or rehearsals, the promenaders, as they passed, would say, "Ah! Mrs. Merry is at the theatre; there is her chariot." . . . Having transacted her morning business at the dramatic temple, Mrs. M. would resume her chariot seat, and pay her morning visits to some of the first families of the city. Often in our walks, we have seen this vehicle standing before the doors of some of our most respectable and intellectual citizens.[60]

When the Chestnut Street company reassembled in Baltimore in order to fulfill its usual fall engagement there, Mrs. Wignell probably was not on hand to witness the debuts of new additions, including one of the best-known names in American theatre history, Joseph Jefferson. In addition, Twaits, another excellent burletta singer recruited from England by Wood, helped to compensate for the loss of Bernard. "These able accessions to the company made it very powerful in comedy. Jefferson,

[59] *Ibid.*, Chap. XXXII, December 10, 1854.
[60] *Ibid.*

Twaits, Blissett, Warren and Wood, constituted an unparalleled combination."[61]

Mrs. Wignell appeared for the first time after the birth of her daughter on November 11, in Baltimore. Within the next month she gradually resumed her place in the company, giving seven performances in seven different roles before the close of the engagement.

Although the Philadelphia season opened on December 12, she did not perform until the following week. Appearing for the first time at the Chestnut Street theatre since her husband's death, she was welcomed by "votaries of elegance and fashion. . . . The area of the boxes was a galaxy at once brilliant and cheering. Indeed every part of the house was 'filled to overflowing.' This circumstance may be regarded as an act of homage to the superior talents and elegance of the Lady Manager."[62] For the occasion she chose her most famous and popular role of Juliet, described as "one unbroken stream of splendid passion." The evening must have been a poignant and gratifying one to her because the audience welcoming her return was so large that it brought box office receipts of $1,145, one of the highest totals for the year. As the season advanced, Mrs. Wignell resumed what was for her a more normal burden of performances. During her first year as manager and actress she presented approximately twenty-seven roles in fifty-one appearances, a significant increase over thirty-eight of the previous year. Affairs of the company seemed to prosper under the new management and the directress must have been grateful with what appeared to have been a successful operation.

The most significant event that spring (ultimately affecting Mrs. Wignell's future) was the death of Warren's wife Anne, "greatly lamented on account of her worth and virtues."[63] In his March 10 entry in his journal, however, Warren reveals a matter-of-fact reaction to her death as well as his inherent practicality:

---

[61] *Ibid.*, Chap. XXXVII, January 14, 1855.
[62] Philadelphia *Gazette*, December 20, 1803.
[63] Durang, "The Philadelphia Stage," Chap. XXXVII, January 14, 1855.

"This morning between 10—and 11—Mrs. Anne Warren died—she has been ailing for 4 months but latterly her health appeared to improve—she took a [?] cold about a week ago which brought on a Relapse—that terminated her existence—May she rest in peace—our connexion began about thirteen years ago—she has left me one Child—the only one we ever had—My Benefit which was to have been tonight—on this event taking place—is postponed." These seemingly detached remarks, in strong contrast to Warren's grief-stricken response to his second wife's death, suggest that his first marriage was not a particularly close one. But it was not until more than two years later that Mrs. Wignell and Warren, widow and widower, married.

During the Baltimore season Mrs. Wignell probably appeared in as many as sixteen different roles in seventeen performances. In June a "detachment of the company" returned to Philadelphia and after a series of delays, finally began a short engagement at the Southwark Theatre. "The whole strength of the company seemed to be there with the exception of Mrs. Wignell," who undoubtedly rested for a few months while Warren tried to find audiences to sustain the company through the summer. After only six performances in Philadelphia between June 25 and July 18, the thespians sought playgoers in Annapolis. Low box-office receipts indicate a discouraging reception. Warren next attempted to procure the ballroom again in "Marlbro" but "Dr. Beams who had the letting of that Edifice was inexorable." Instead Warren obtained Mr. McLaughlin's ballroom in George Town, where the company shared the modest profits for four weeks, returning to Baltimore on October 1 in time to commence its fall engagement.[64]

Because of ill health Mrs. Wignell did not make an appearance until October 19. She explained in a letter to a friend in Philadelphia:

Baltimore, October 4, 1804

My very good Friend
    I look forward with the expectation and hope of seeing you in

Philadelphia early in the first week of December—you will think I have given you timely notice, but as the bedroom is to be white-washed and the other papered for my health's sake, I write a month before as now I shall be certain the apartment must be free from damp.

I have had a sad and sorry time this fall, confined three weeks to the house by illness, ten days of that time I was extremely ill and many of those days, in danger. I do not yet feel like myself, but hope the journey and change of air will make me quite well.

Elizabeth, thank God, is in fine health and spirits and is grown a lovely girl, I think she will amuse us many an hour when we get together. I am sure she would send you a kiss if she knew how for she has a sweet temper, and a most affectionate heart. You will love her very much.

I must thank you to look for me a clean and good girl to take care of my rooms before I come home as it will be a great comfort to have some person ready to attend me on my arrival, but I will send a line to inform you of the exact time when you may expect to see me—'til when, beieve [*sic*] me to be

> Your sincere friend
> and well wishes
> (signed)   Anne Wignell

The business of the Theatre has been and is very, very bad indeed.[65]

Warren also complained that the season, in general, was "a very sickly one—most of the company is indisposed at one time or another. This town [is] thin of inhabitants in consequence of its unhealthiness."[66] Throughout the fall engagement box-office receipts reflected this unhealthiness, sometimes necessitating salary cuts of one-half and one-fourth.

When the company opened in Philadelphia, Anne embarked on one of the busiest seasons of her career. In addition to her managerial duties she probably played more parts in one year than ever before: approximately forty-one roles in ninety-one performances. As well as being one of the most challenging years in quantity of work, undoubtedly it was also one of her most

[65] Letter from Anne Wignell to Mrs. Thackerson. A copy of this letter is in the Alexandria Public Library.
[66] Warren, Journals, October 20, 1804.

challenging in quality. She not only appeared in nine different Shakespearean roles but she also played many other popular characterizations of the period, including Almeria, Palmira, Calista, Belvidera, Leonora, Roxana, Hermione, Lady Teazle, Amanthis, Mrs. Haller, Lady Eleanor Irwin, Cora, Emma, Amelrosa, and Rosamunda. This brilliant display of Anne's repertoire was made possible largely by the availability of a leading actor equal to her powers, Thomas Cooper, who returned from England in November. After a successful run in New York, Cooper filled an equally successful engagement in Philadelphia between December 29 and January 26. Joining with Cooper for ten of his first eleven appearances, Mrs. Wignell often pushed box-office receipts to more than nine hundred dollars. She was especially effective as Ophelia on December 31 when "many an uplifted handkerchief, and many a streaming eye, bespoke the surpassing charms . . ." of her portrayal.[67] Of the series, the most significant one for Mrs. Wignell was her "cold, inanimate and dispirited" Lady Macbeth on January 16. Although the newspaper does not announce it as her first portrayal of the role, no other earlier record of her performing this famous characterization remains. Wood asserts that Mrs. Wignell had previously "declined playing the Lady, on the plea that Mrs. Siddon's representation of the part had left an impression on her mind, dispiriting to any effort at competition or success"; he also mistakenly adds that it was "a resolution I do not recollect her ever abandoning."[68] Perhaps the actress temporarily agreed with Wood, who thought her reluctance as "a strange diffidence, when we recollect that Mrs. Wignell's estimation in London was by no means confined to the gentler characters, but was extended even to the most powerful, as Calista, Hermione, Roxana, Horatia and others." One contemporary theatregoer agreed with Wood: "Whatever Mrs. Wignell may suppose of her *forte* being in the pathetic and tender, we believe it lays where violence is required, where the conflict of the

[67] Philadelphia *Gazette*, December 31, 1804.
[68] Wood, *Personal Recollections*, 105.

passions and the ragings of the soul are to be pourtrayed—."[69] Certainly, however, Anne finally determined that she was better suited to the loving, although passionate, heroines than the strong, forceful types such as Lady Macbeth, for that role never became a staple in her repertoire.

In spite of its spectacular offerings that winter, the theatre could not consistently draw Philadelphians to brave an "uncommonly severe" winter with its attendant snow and Chestnut Street quagmires.[70] Accordingly the management announced that in "consequence of the disappointment which many persons experienced in being prevented (through the inclemency of the weather, during the last three weeks) attending the Theatre—the Managers have extended their engagement with *Mr. Cooper to four nights more.*"[71] Box-office receipts for the entire fifteen-night engagement ranged from a low of $258 to a high of $1,307 (on the occasion of Cooper's benefit) giving an average of $758 per evening for the run. Having temporarily exhausted the available audience, the theatre's receipts plunged to $79 the night after Cooper's last appearance, and with the exception of a highly successful benefit for the poor which drew $1,012, the company, bereft of its star attraction, could not draw a house worth more than $330 during the next two weeks. The managers responded with a suggestion to close the theatre for a week.[72] But when "The Company prevailed on them to continue—and the company take the risk," the managers consented. Revenues continued to remain quite low until the beginning of the benefits, but even then Anne earned only $621, one of her smallest American receipts. Thus, the busy Philadelphia season of 1804–1805 must have concluded on an anxious note for her. In addition to the distressing "feast or famine" box office and the exhausting schedule, she "had been a good deal annoyed in the business of the theatre; some of the actors pressed their affairs with ungentleness." Mrs. Wignell, "a

[69] *Ibid.*; Philadelphia *Gazette*, December 18, 1805.
[70] Warren, Journals, January 19, 1805.
[71] Philadelphia, *United States Gazette*, January 21, 1805.
[72] Warren, Journals, February 16, 1805.

sensitive, generous and confiding woman," lacked sufficient firmness to conduct a company "where a variety of dispositions are to be met, jealousies are to be soothed and intrigues are to be counteracted."[73] These converging factors must have persuaded her to turn over the management to William Warren even before the company moved to Baltimore for its spring engagement.[74] Warren briefly noted the arrangement on April 3, 1805: "Mrs. Wignell made a proposal to me to . . . Receive her share of the lease—I agreed to accept the same—before leaving the City—the Agents —John Ashley and Chas. Biddle executed the transfer in my favour—I assume the Debts of the firm to be Warren and Reinagle—" And almost in confirmation of the authority of his new position, he made the additional notation, "I project a voyage to England."[75]

However, he did not leave for England until after he had established the company in the Baltimore theatre and had engaged Thomas Cooper once again to give a boost to the spring season. The visiting actor increased box-office totals by approximately one-third, which may have persuaded the management to extend his engagement until June 10. But the novelty of the guest performer soon wore off and receipts returned to their usual average. Nevertheless Cooper provided Anne with another extended opportunity to present some of her most famous roles. In the meantime Warren sailed for England, returning in time to welcome his troupe to Baltimore on October 1.

During Warren's absence the "company played in Washington City and Alexandria,"[76] while Mrs. Wignell, joined with Cooper, undertook her first New York appearance since 1802. Together the popular team appeared for six nights in established favorites: *The Fair Penitent, The Orphan, Romeo and Juliet, Hamlet,*

[73] *Ibid.*, Durang, "The Philadelphia Stage," Chap. XXXIX, January 28, 1855.
[74] Charles Durang suggests that Mrs. Wignell, "in order to give the right government of the company to one more resolute than herself, . . . married again." Warren's journal indicates, however, that she relinquished the management a year before she married Warren.
[75] Warren, Journals, April 3, 1805.
[76] Durang, "The Philadelphia Stage," Chap. XXXVIII, January 21, 1855.

Pizarro, The Rival Queens, and *The Sultan.* Although Mrs. Wignell had just experienced an arduous year, that challenging schedule probably had the positive effect of putting her in excellent
condition, allowing for maximum flexibility and control in voice
and body. These advantages, combined with her sensitivity and
deepened emotional range, must have resulted in the ultimate of
artistry, for her acting drew superlative praises. A local critic wrote
that as Calista, "Her fine silver tone voice . . . in full volumn [*sic*]
and accompanied by her peculiar grace of action, made, as it has
always done, an impression such as no other actress in this country could ever make." After her second performance, in which
she portrayed Monimia, the critic again wrote: "When we say
we do not think we ever saw Mrs. Wignell play better, it may be
readily believed it approached the perfection of histrionic art.
Her powers are in full maturity and she gave us last night their
best exertion. Who that once has seen her wondrous exhibitions,
can afterwards receive any satisfaction from the attempts of any
other actress in a similar line that the American Theatre can
boast of?" An equally appreciative audience "bore universal testimony to her extraordinary powers" as Ophelia, termed "the most
chaste, highly finished, and exquisite piece of scenic representation we ever witnessed. . . . In the distressing mad scene she almost surpassed expectation and though no professed singer, yet
the soft and plaintive melody of her simple tones was in the
highest degree impressive and affecting."[77] At the conclusion of
the successful engagement Mrs. Wignell probably retreated to
Annapolis during the remaining summer months for a much-
deserved rest. She was still there on September 20 when Warren
arrived from England. On the following day the returning traveler wrote in his diary: "I take a gig—and go out to Mr. Wharfs at
the Red Lion—12 miles to see Mrs. W—." And the next day he
added: "I spend the day at Mr. Wharfs." These entries are the
first in the journal which suggest that one year later the friends of
ten years' standing would join together their personal as well as
their professional lives.

[77] New York *Evening Post,* June 25, 27, July 2, 1805.

VI

Mrs. Wignell Becomes Mrs. Warren
1805-1808

The recurrence of yellow fever during the summer of 1805 delayed the fall theatre season. Fearing an outbreak similar to the one in Philadelphia, Baltimore officials would not allow the theatre to open. Warren believed that "the Board of Health wou'd prevent our opening altogether if they dared."[1] But on Monday, October 7, the Chestnut Street company embarked on one of its most successful years, with "crouded houses" as "convincing proofs, that whilst the managers exert themselves to procure meritorious performers, the citizens of Baltimore will liberally reward them."[2] Two new actresses provided relief for Mrs. Wignell in carrying the responsibilities of leading roles. Mrs. Melmoth (from New York) engaged in "the heavy leading business," whereas Mrs. Woodham (from England) strengthened the musical and comic pieces.[3] Undoubtedly Mrs. Wignell was grateful that the actresses helped reduce the number of appearances by almost one-third compared to the previous year. Although Durang says Mrs. Wignell acted only "whenever the casts of the pieces suited her,"[4] during the season of 1805–1806 she gave sixty-six performances in thirty-five different roles (compared to approximately forty-one roles the year before), seven of them new to her.

If the year was less strenuous in the total number of appearances, it was nevertheless one of the most interesting and chal-

---

[1] Warren, Journals, October 1, 1805.
[2] Baltimore *American*, November 28, 1805.
[3] Durang, "The Philadelphia Stage," Chap. XXXIX, January 28, 1855.
[4] *Ibid.*

lenging in her career. The addition of Mrs. Melmouth provided her with the opportunity to share leading roles in *The Distressed Mother, Mary Queen of Scots, The Earl of Essex,* and *Pizarro.*[5] Also, both Fennell and Cooper made separate guest appearances during the winter which afforded Mrs. Wignell further opportunity to play some of her most demanding and successful characterizations. Before concluding the Baltimore season she participated in two new productions. The first, James Cobb's adaptation of *The Wife of Two Husbands* (from the "popular melo-drama" by Pixérecourt) was successful enough to be produced in Philadelphia later.[6] After the other work, *Mary Queen of Scots* by St. John, concluded the fall engagement on November 28, a local critic offered a lengthy tribute to Mrs. Wignell:

> Were my talents adequate to the task, the fascinating Mrs. Wignell should excite my warmest praise for the enraptured & sublime pleasure I have often experienced in witnessing her propriety of action, vivacious countenance, harmonious voice, and truly impressive elocution:—he must be dead to every generous sentiment, and fine feeling of nature, who does not, after seeing her perform, retire from the theatre with improved sensibility, and a heart expanding with social virtue and affection. Who that has seen her angelic countenance, in the Grecian Daughter when she enters after reanimating her almost lifeless father, but sighs to have such a child; what parent but must ejaculate a wish for so lovely a preserver from tyranic rage—Many, very many years may she, with unimpaired powers, receive the well earned plaudits of admiring Americans.[7]

On November 30 Anne with Elizabeth and her nurse and several other actors departed from Baltimore in a stagecoach chartered by Warren.[8] Arriving in Philadelphia on Sunday, the actors opened the theatre on the following evening; but Mrs. Wignell did not make her winter debut until December 11, when she appeared as Lady Teazle in *The School for Scandal.* This performance provided the first opportunity for the "Censor," an

[5] Wood, *Personal Recollections,* 109.
[6] Baltimore *American,* November 22, 1805.
[7] *Ibid.,* November 28, 1805.
[8] Warren, Journals, November 30, 1805.

anonymous critic, to evaluate Mrs. Wignell's acting for the newly established journal the *Theatrical Censor*. Noteworthy because he claimed to have known the actress as Miss Brunton, his comments testify to the effects of time and to her durability as an artist: "When we first knew Mrs. Wignell she was Miss Brunton, of Covent Garden Theatre; the delight of youth, and the admiration of age. We see her altered, indeed, in person; but not a spark of her attraction as an actress seems extinct. *Lady Teazle* may not fear the efforts of *Backbite*, nor the insinuations of *Sneerwell*." Most of that critic's subsequent comments concerning her acting that winter were also favorable. As Mary, Queen of Scots, she "was very fine"; her Ophelia, performed in her "best style," was "wonderfully tender and impressive"; and her portrayal of the queen in *Richard III*, "was entitled to full commendation." He also appreciated her benefit portrayal of the tamed shrew Juliana, "(with a song in character)," in a new work, *The Honey Moon*, obviously borrowed from Shakespeare by John Tobin. Nevertheless the critic found fault with her portrayal of Desdemona because she "did not look, nor speak," like the Moor's bride. He also observed that "Mrs. Wignell makes *treeüly* of *truly, bleeii* of *blue*."[9]

Neither the brief criticism nor the repertoire suggests any new turns in Anne's career this year, although her appearances with Fennell and Cooper highlighted her schedule and helped to make the whole season "one of extraordinary success."[10] Making his first appearance in Philadelphia since the time of Wignell's death, Fennell began his twelve-night engagement on January 20, in one of his most acclaimed roles, Zanga (*The Revenge*). Out of his fifteen performances, Mrs. Wignell appeared with her old stage friend ten times in works in which they both had become acclaimed: *Hamlet, The Gamester, The Voice of Nature, Othello, Alexander the Great, Richard III, Isabella, The Castle Spectre,*

---

[9] *Theatrical Censor*, December 11, 1805, p. 18–19; January 15, 1805, p. 73; January 22, 1805, p. 82; February 12, 1806, p. 111; February 24, 1806, p. 125; February 3, 1806, p. 104, 105.
[10] Durang, "The Philadelphia Stage," Chap. XXXIX, January 28, 1855.

Venice Preserv'd, and *The Earl of Essex.* Fennell's entire run drew substantial houses, the greatest one on the night of the benefit for the orphaned children of John Hodgkinson, who had died the previous summer of yellow fever in Washington, D.C. One week after Fennell's last appearance on February 24, Mrs. Wignell began the benefit season, which lasted until March 15 when Warren "bought Mrs. [*sic*] Francis, Blissett and McKenzie's benefits to make room for an engagement . . . with Cooper—to conclude the season."[11] Of his nine performances, Anne appeared with him in seven productions, five of them repetitions of dramas in which she had acted a few months earlier with Fennell: *Hamlet, The Gamester, Othello, Richard III,* and *The Castle Spectre.* Unfortunately Cooper's engagement was not as financially successful as Fennell's, which had averaged $626 a night (exclusive of the Hodgkinson benefit). In contrast, Cooper's appearances averaged only $386. His disappointing audiences might be attributed to Fennell's offering a series of readings and recitation at the university on Tuesday and Thursday evenings.[12] In addition, Warren believed that "Fennell has been of great injury to these nights by starting a parcel of lies—among the rest that I would not let him play with Cooper when C. J. Ingersoll proposed it from Cooper and myself and he [Fennell] refused."[13] If Cooper felt chagrin over the situation, he must have appreciated a benefit of $1,002, which eclipsed Fennell's night by approximately $150.

Following the conclusion of Cooper's engagement on March 31, the Chestnut Street company performed one more week in Philadelphia before moving to Baltimore for the spring season. Mrs. Wignell and Warren traveled to Maryland together but in separate conveyances, he is his gig and she in "W Ryans coach."[14]

During the thirty-four nights of performances between April 12 and June 10, Mrs. Wignell appeared fourteen times in the

---

[11] Warren, *Journals,* March 15, 1806.
[12] *Port Folio,* March 22, 1806, p. 172.
[13] Warren, *Journals,* March 29, 1806.
[14] *Ibid.,* April 11, 1806.

most successful productions carried over from the Philadelphia season. The most popular attraction, *The Honey Moon*, warranted five performances and two reviews from the local critics. Believing that Anne was ill suited to the role of Juliana (based on Shakespeare's Kate), one reviewer commented she "was *out of her element* in Juliana: And yet to say so is no disparagement to that admirable woman. She was born to tread the boards in a high sphere of acting; and the greatness of her mind will never permit her to excel in a lowly state . . . yet much of the character of the reformation of Juliana was lost in the naturally majestic appearance of Mrs. Wignell."[15] Another critic, satisfied with her performance, did not believe it necessary to discuss it in detail, for "all that . . . [he] could say, would not increase her theatrical reputation."[16] The first review suggests that as Anne matured in age and appearance, she seems to have assumed a more majestic bearing, which must have compensated for her short stature, a disadvantage frequently noted during her English career but seldom alluded to after she came to the United States.

At the conclusion of the successful spring engagement, Mrs. Wignell probably vacationed at Barney's Red Lion ("the house formerly kept by Mr. Wharf")[17] for the summer months, while Warren accompanied his troupe to Philadelphia, where they shared profits of an eight-night run between June 18 and July 9. The company also performed in Alexandria during July, August, and September, but Warren appeared with them only sporadically and took "no share" because he did not "wish to stay with the Company—any longer than convenient."[18] He probably wanted to spend as much time as possible with Anne. He leaves no record of when they decided to marry, although during the week he spent in Baltimore he made a provocative journal entry: "Saturday, July 19, the day I can't forget." A few days later he joined the company in Alexandria, but on August 14 he received a letter

---

[15] Baltimore *American*, April 24, 1806.
[16] *Ibid.*, April 29, 1806.
[17] Warren, Journals, July 11, 1806.
[18] *Ibid.*, July 23, 1806.

from Anne urging him to return to Baltimore because of the illness of his daughter Nancy.[19] When he arrived there on the following day, he found her "much better—almost well."[20] He then
most likely remained in Baltimore until August 28, when he was
"united to Mrs. Anne Wignell by the Reverend Dr. Ratoone, at
Mr. Wharfes who was present together with . . . Alexander
Rienagle [sic]—Mrs. Wharfe & Miss Brewer—." Following the
ceremony, the wedding party dined at "McKoys 14 miles from
Baltimore."[21] From there the Warrens proceeded in his gig to
Vansville where they remained until September 12. They also
spent a few days in George Town while Warren checked on his
company in Alexandria, but they finally returned to Baltimore
to prepare for the opening of the fall season, October 1, 1806.[22]

Durang has revealed that "there was some surprise expressed,"
over the Wignell-Warren marriage, but he does not disclose the
nature of the surprise.[23] To some, Warren obviously did not appear as a likely husband for Anne Wignell. Such sentiments were
expressed as late as 1811 by George Frederick Cooke, the visiting
British star, who explained to Dunlap: "So , . . . this is the widow's
third choice. he [sic] is not the Warren I remember in England.
What a fop he is. did [sic] you notice the tassels to his garters? I
never saw anybody else wear them. Upon my word the good lady
seems to descend with every husband: first Merry, then Wignell
& then Warren!"[24] Other descriptions of Warren made by those
long associated with him in America suggest that although he
did not make as forceful an impression as Wignell, the two men
were similar in nature. Dunlap remembered Warren "as a pleas-
ant companion and an upright man," and Fennell identified him
as "a man of honour and of trust . . . his name is fixed on a firm
base of general integrity." Wood, his partner for sixteen years,
knew him as an "easy mild tempered man," who "loved and re-

---

[19] *Ibid.*, August 14, 1806.
[20] *Ibid.*, August 15, 1806.
[21] *Ibid.*, August 28, 1806.
[22] *Ibid.*, September 12, 18, 1806.
[23] Durang, "The Philadelphia Stage," Chap. XXXIX, January 28, 1855.
[24] Dunlap, *Diary*, II, 419.

spected his profession, and was willing at all times to favor the efforts of deserving novices by freely aiding them with the result of his own experience."[25] Such descriptions suggest that Warren and Mrs. Wignell were suited to each other in temperament and values. Drawn together by long and close association, they had not only embarked on American theatrical careers at the same time, but also they had remained with the same company for ten years. During that time they had shared the successes and failures of the Chestnut Street company, as well as their own personal misfortunes and now each needed a parent for an orphaned child. Anne Wignell, at thirty-seven, undoubtedly had decided to remain in the United States, content to share the rest of her life with the man who had become one of her oldest and closest associates.

Mrs. Warren made her first appearance under her new name in Baltimore on October 8, when she initiated an even busier year than the one before. During 1806–1807 she appeared in approximately forty roles in seventy-three productions. Again her schedule included Shakespearean, Restoration, and eighteenth century tragedies, as well as sentimental comedies and melodramas. Fennell's two-month engagement enabled her to perform twelve of her most admired roles (including nine tragedies, two melodramas, and one comedy), and her starring engagement in New York during March brought the total number of her tragic roles for the year to seventeen. Of the six new characterizations she learned that year, Anne tried two of them for the first time in Baltimore. As Lady Transit in Richard Cumberland's comedy *A Hint to Husbands*, Mrs. Warren embodied "—the look, the manner, the feelings of an injured but forgiving wife," giving "energy to rectitude of life," and depicting "the charms of wedded felicity in all their effulgence."[26] But neither this comedy nor the other new play, *The School for Friends*, was sufficiently popular to become a stock piece in the company repertoire.

---

[25] Dunlap, *History of the American Theatre,* I, 368; Fennell, *An Apology for . . . James Fennell,* 405; Wood, *Personal Recollections,* 113; 328.
[26] Baltimore *American,* November 21, 1806.

At the conclusion of a successful but uneventful fall season, the Warrens returned to Philadelphia to a rented house on Sansom Street,[27] which later became Mrs. Warren's Philadelphia home until she died.[28] As the Warrens settled into their new domestic life and a prosperous season, they encountered considerable professional criticism in the pages of the *United States Gazette.* Mrs. Warren's performance as Lady Teazle in the opening production of the winter season signaled the first attack which appeared on December 3 in a review of *The School for Scandal:*

> Lady Teazle was done by Mrs. Warren (as I think she is called *this* winter) in a manner, to speak most favorably of it, only tolerable. This lady is highly and justly celebrated for the excellence of her performance in characters to which her talents are adapted. But that of Lady Teazle is quite out of her walk. However, as it would probably cost the manager money to procure variety of talents adapted to the various characters to be represented, the town must acquiesce. We have to thank him for one indulgence. It is said that he has engaged Mr. Fennell for the *latter part of the season,* so that we shall probably have the pleasure of seeing him for a few evenings upon the boards, unless it should be found that the house can be filled without him.[29]

As might be expected, a champion, "A Friend to Justice," rose to the defense of the Warrens and subsequent issues of the paper printed a flurry of letters over anonymous signatures which defended and attacked the Warrens. Waged in waspish language, the controversy narrowed to two basic issues: (1) Warren was accused of providing inferior theatrical offerings because he refused to employ a variety of quality performers. Specifically, he

[27] Warren, Journals, November 30, 1806.
[28] See the *Philadelphia Directory* for the years 1807 and 1808. This house became the property of Mrs. Warren's daughter and her husband Peter Benson. One of twenty-two row houses built shortly after 1800 from plans by Thomas Carstairs, the dwelling was three and a half stories in height with two rooms to a floor. See George Tatum, *Penn's Great Town: 250 Years of Philadelphia Architecture* (Philadelphia, 1961), 47–48. A detailed description of the house written for a Mutual Insurance policy issued to Benson in 1825, suggests that the Warrens enjoyed a home of quiet elegance requiring three to five servants for maintenance.
[29] Philadelphia, *United States Gazette,* December 3, 1806. See also subsequent December issues: 8, 10, 11, 13, 15, 17, 18.

refused to hire Mrs. Whitlock—and possibly Mrs. Marshall, who had become Mrs. Wilmot—as well as refusing to engage Fennell until mid-season when the box office would need fresh stimulus. (2) The implied basis for these decisions was the professional jealousy of Mrs. Warren, supposedly fearful of competition. As interpreted from the opposite point of view, these accusations were the backlash from disappointed performers.

Although the accusations from both sides may have been grounded in truth, the validity of the charges is difficult to determine. Only the outcome of the dispute is clear: (1) Fennell began his engagement in December instead of later in the season. (2) Mrs. Whitlock was not hired but Mrs. Wilmot was engaged for the following summer. Although of no great consequence, the controversy gives insight into the professional problems which Anne may have created or encountered. Viewed from the vantage of more than 160 years, her position in 1806 as "unquestionably the best actress that ever graced the American stage"[30] appears so indisputable that it is difficult to believe that she had cause to feel professional jealously. At the same time, her acknowledged artistic superiority and her influential position in the foremost theatre company of the country must have caused jealously in others. Certainly she was the favored actress of the company and she likely had first choice of the new roles and the option on the long-established ones. Being in the same company with her may have been a distinct disadvantage to an aspiring actress and may have been the reason why Mrs. Whitlock and Mrs. Wilmot withdrew from the company. But in 1806 both of these actresses apparently sought employment with Warren, and if their rejection was the source of personal as well as professional attacks on the Warrens, it is perhaps understandable, however regrettable.

In spite of the critical attacks on the management, some of the articles and letters included restrained praise for Mrs. Warren's acting. Her portrayal of Ophelia was "charmingly performed. . . . We have rarely seen as good performance as Mrs. Warren's

[30] *Ibid.*, December 18, 1806.

Ophelia." In *King Lear,* her "new-fangled Cordelia, was engaging and correct." But one letter written in the midst of the heated exchange attacked her acting in general:

> Mrs. Warren may be a good performer in some characters, but they are not those in which she usually appears on stage. To those characters which require little study and less intellect to represent properly, she is certainly equal but if you take from her a melodious voice, and an action, graceful without being often correct, she possesses no one requisite to represent those characters which she attempts to perform. If we are to judge from her performance, she does not understand the characters of Shakespeare [for] she perpetually misplaces emphasis and mistakes the author's sense.[31]

How justified the criticism was cannot be determined, but it is out of tune with most of the judgments of her acting. But at the same time, Mrs. Warren's interpretations were challenged also by "Gregory Gryphon" writing for the *Theatrical Censor and the Critical Miscellany.* He objected to her "very unnecessary hoydenness" as Lady Teazle in the second act of *The School for Scandal,* and to her "equally misplaced affectation of the idiot and gawky" in the apartments of Joseph Surface.[32] Making one of the few unfavorable evaluations of Mrs. Warren's voice, he described it as "false and wiry,"[33] although he conceded in a later review that it was agreeable "whenever she uses her own voice as she did in Agatha [*Lover's Vows*]."[34] After her appearance as Mrs. Greville in *Secrets Worth Knowing,* he termed the role "unworthy" of Mrs. Warren's talents, an observation which undoubtedly could be offered concerning a great number of her roles.[35]

On February 14, one week after Fennell's engagement ended, Mrs. Warren was engaged to perform in New York with Thomas

[31] *Ibid.,* December 20, 29, 11, 1806.
[32] *Theatrical Censor and Critical Miscellany,* December 6, 1806, p. 163.
[33] *Ibid.,* 161.
[34] *Ibid.,* December 13, 1806, p. 187.
[35] *Ibid.,* December 6, 1806, p. 168.

Cooper. She left Philadelphia two days later, accompanied by Warren's brother Phillip, for what was to be her final starring engagement in New York.[36] Her schedule included some of her most admired characterizations: Calista, Isabella, Alicia, Elvira, Mrs. Beverly, Roxana, and Euphrasia. Following the unpleasant controversy in Philadelphia it must have been gratifying for her to find "very crowded" houses in New York and a "boundless solicitude for tickets of admission . . . throughout the period of . . . her engagement."[37] In *The Fair Penitent*, her first performance of the run, she was half of an "extraordinary treat . . . supported as it was by the united powers of Mr. Cooper and Mrs. Warren." Her own singular powers captivated the critic: "Those well-remembered tones—those eloquent pauses—that graceful motion—that expressive countenance—all spoke to us in a language that is never conveyed to us by any other human being. The unbroken silence —the fast-falling tear—the dejection of the head and countenance, were the involuntary tributes to her superior excellence that were offered her in every part of the house. Never have we seen even Mrs. Warren play so well, or with so much effect."[38]

Her second appearance, as Isabella, "displayed Mrs. Warren in truly captivating colours," although "Zoilus," the critic for the *Evening Post*, was less enthusiastic about the rest of the production: "When she divests herself of her ring, when she meets *Biron* for the second time, when she bursts into solitary ravings, and when she struggles against those who attempt to tear her from the dead body, and calls on *Biron* to assist her, every heart pays her the homage of the truest praise . . . . Those who went to see Mrs. Warren were indeed gratified; but, those who went to see *the play*, had much to pardon." The critic treated the remaining performances in less detail and often with less extravagant praise. Although Anne's "very superior talents" highlighted the production of *Jane Shore* and her Alicia was an "excellent performance," in "certain parts, she made rather too much use of

[36] Warren, Journals, February 16, 1807.
[37] New York *Evening Post*, March 3, 1807.
[38] *Ibid.*, February 20, 1807.

the powers of her voice." In *Pizarro* she had "no great opportunity" as Elvira "to make any strong impression" but "her final scene was given with interest and dignity." In the last part of *The Gamester* "Mrs. Warren frequently charmed with genuine expressions of tenderness and affliction," and her "haughty jealousy" as Statira in *Alexander the Great* "produced a strong impression."[39] For her last appearance she performed the part of Euphrasia, the role in which she had made her original debut in England and had continued to perform successfully for twenty-two years. The next day, March 7, she returned to Philadelphia with $1,300 profit.[40] Taking no more than a day to rest from her trip, she resumed her regular performance duties with her own company as Cora in *Virgin of the Sun,* and subsequently learned three new roles and gave fifteen performances before the company moved to Baltimore. Undoubtedly Mrs. Warren was grateful that the spring engagement, unlike the winter one in Philadelphia, passed for her without unpleasant incident. Perhaps one of the most noteworthy events of the spring was the benefit for the actor and former manager of the Old American Company, Lewis Hallam, who had recently returned to Philadelphia "determined to seek, in the scene of his youth and his celebrity, an asylum for the infirmities of age, and the adversities of fortune."[41] His appearance of April 15 as Lord Olgeby in *The Clandestine Marriage* brought a tribute of $819.66 to the old stage veteran.

Two days after closing the Philadelphia theatre, Warren traveled to Baltimore "in a Carriage which I had built for my wife's use," arriving on the same day that he opened the theatre, April 23. Mrs. Warren did not perform until May, participating in only about one-third of the performances during the engagement. On June 14 the Warrens again returned to Philadelphia in their own carriage by the circuitous route of York and Lancaster, "intending to recreate—and take our time—and also for the Benefit of the

39 *Ibid.,* February 23, 25, 27, March 3, 1807.
40 Warren, Journals, March 7, 1807.
41 Philadelphia, *Poulson's American Daily Advertiser,* April 15, 1807.

children's Health—the first part of it was very unpleasant—the Roads and Inns being so wretched—the latter very pleasant."[42]

As had been her custom for several summers, Mrs. Warren did not join the company in Philadelphia. Set up on the sharing plan for "8 nights only," its schedule featured plays prominent in the repertoire of Mrs. Wilmot, who had returned to the company. Mrs. Warren interrupted her summer rest for one performance on the occasion of the benefit for the widow and orphans of Robert Wilson, a company carpenter killed during the season in Baltimore. Subject to fits, the unfortunate man "was seized with one while up in the flies—he fell on the stage and fractured his scull [sic]."[43] On the night of the benefit, the entire cast volunteered their performances, with Anne performing as Juliana in the popular comedy The Honey Moon.

For the rest of the summer the Warrens appear to have been free from professional pressures and concerns. However, in August, they suffered a personal loss when Warren's five-year old daughter Nancy "was attacked with dysentery—which in seventeen days—deprived me that Sweet Child."[44] Immediately following the funeral the grief-stricken Warren took his wife and Elizabeth on a five-day excursion about the Philadelphia vicinity. They spent several days at Chestnut Hill and returned home on September 8. Remaining in Philadelphia only one week, the Warrens sought the distraction of additional travel and subsequently set out on a ten-day trip of 218 miles, touring as far north as Bethlehem (where they examined the Young Ladies School) and as far west as Hanover. They finally arrived in Baltimore, where they rented a "small house by Grays Gardens and furnished the same."[45]

Anne's last year of performance followed the pattern of the past few years. She maintained a moderately heavy schedule

---

[42] Warren, Journals, April 25, June 20, 1807.
[43] Ibid., June 22, July 8, 1807.
[44] Ibid., September, 1807.
[45] Ibid., September 8, 25, 1807.

(about fifty-seven performances of thirty-four roles) consisting of a mixture of tragedies, comedies, and melodramas. Enjoying once again the support of visiting tragedian Thomas Cooper, she performed mostly from her tragic repertoire. Nothing in the busy, successful year seemed to suggest that soon her thriving career would end.

Mrs. Warren interrupted the routine of the fall season with her first and only engagement in Boston between November 20 and December 4. Scheduled for six nights and a benefit, she performed some of her most popular roles: Belvidera, Euphrasia, Lady Teazle, Isabella, Elvira, Calista and Juliet. Unhappily for theatregoers, her engagement was not well publicized until it was half over.[46] Although only a handful of spectators attended her opening performance as Belvidera, the local critic was so impressed that he initiated a publicity campaign in her behalf.[47] He praised "not only the language of the most ardent, pure, and unchangeable affection, but the expressive looks, the expressive gestures, and those thrilling tones which give an '*echo to the very seat where love does sit enthron'd;*' yet without rant, without violence, without tearing the lungs, or distorting the limbs."[48] Another critic indicated that the years had added pounds to Anne's figure and that her voice was not always under control.

> Mrs. Warren's person is inclining to corpulency, and her face perhaps from this circumstance, is not well suited to the expression of sorrow; though the emotions of astonishment, joy, hope, and elevation of mind, are finely portrayed by her countenance. Her voice in unimpassioned utterance is delightfully harmonious and clear; but in violent exclamation it wants volume, and becomes rather shrill and unpleasant. . . . The emphasis of this lady is in general, remarkably correct and impressive; and the business of the scene is conducted by her with uncommon ease of execution. Her action is peculiarly graceful and appropriate. But she is apt to overstrain her voice, which, while it spoils its harmony, is

---

[46] Michael, "A History of the Professional Theatre in Boston from the Beginning to 1816," 549.

[47] *Ibid.*, 550.

[48] *Ibid.*, Michael cites the Boston *Gazette*, November 23, 1807.

often liable to break in upon the beauty of the sentence, by too abrupt a descent in the transition of her utterance.[49]

In addition to the challenge of a new audience and theatre company, she had an opportunity to perform opposite two of her oldest stage colleagues, John Bernard and James Fennell, playing Lady Teazle to Bernard's Sir Peter, and Calista and Juliet to Fennell's Horatio and Romeo. Although audiences were disappointing during the first half of the engagement, on the last three nights Mrs. Warren drew crowded houses, which concluded the run on a successful note and sent her home with $1,350 profit.[50]

Instead of returning to Baltimore, Mrs. Warren rejoined her family in Philadelphia, where the company had opened its winter season on December 7. Perhaps in an attempt to avoid a renewal of the previous year's criticism, Warren got the season off to an auspicious start by engaging Cooper for six nights and a clear benefit.[51] Cooper and Mrs. Warren teamed once again in their most popular combinations: Hamlet and Ophelia, Othello and Desdemona, Romeo and Juliet, Chamot and Monimia. During the same engagement Cooper performed the role of King Lear for his first time in Philadelphia, supported by Mrs. Warren's Cordelia.[52] The tragedian had no sooner concluded his engagement than Warren offered his audiences another special attraction, this time, comedian John Bernard, who had not appeared in Philadelphia for five years.[53] During his seven-night run Anne performed with her old friend on two occasions, as Lady Teazle and as Lady Eleanor Irwin (*Every One Has His Fault*). After the conclusion of Bernard's appearances, she continued to devote most of her energy to comedies. In *The Merchant of Venice* she performed the role of Portia opposite Lewis Hallman, who had returned again to the Chestnut Street theatre to appear as Shy-

49 *Ibid.*, Michael cites the *Emerald* (n. s.), I (November 28, 1807), 65 f.
50 Warren, Journals, December 13, 1807.
51 "Mr. Cooper's practice at this time was to perform in New York on Monday and Wednesday, and in Philadelphia on Friday and Saturday, which kept him on the road no small portion of the time." Dunlap, *History of the American Theatre*, II, 253.
52 Philadelphia, *United States Gazette*, December 19, 1807.
53 *Ibid.*, January 25, 1807.

lock. He also enjoyed another benefit in April when he played as Mange in *She Stoops to Conquer*.[54]

Of the new plays offered that spring in which Mrs. Warren participated, William Dimond's *Adrian and Orilla* was performed "with a success that established it at once as one of the most admired and productive plays on the list." As had been the case with many popular plays, "it was greatly indebted to the acting of . . . Mrs. Warren as Madame Clermont," as well as to that of Mrs. Wilmot in the role of the page.[55] The winter season concluded on the same high note on which it began, for Cooper returned to Philadelphia for the last four nights (with Anne again supporting him in *Hamlet* and *Othello*) and continued his engagement for nine additional appearances in Baltimore. She joined him in seven of these performances including *Hamlet*, *Wheel of Fortune*, *The Gamester*, *Richard III*, *King Lear*, and *Venice Preserv'd*. "Reiterated shouts of the audience" greeted Mrs. Warren in her first appearance in this, her last Baltimore season. In what was her final performance as Ophelia, "She was remarkably correct, and invariably placed her emphasis with the most critical judgment and precision." She was no less admired as Cordelia, a "character . . . by no means calculated to draw forth the whole of her very superior talents, yet the tenderness and delicacy she diffused over the whole part, presented a beautiful representation of the dutiful and affectionate daughter."[56] Appropriately her last tragic performance was of Belvidera, one of her most lauded roles as a mature artist, and appropriately, too, she performed it with Cooper, one of her most frequent and outstanding stage partners.

During the course of Cooper's engagement, Warren was busy projecting summer plans which necessitated a trip in early May to Alexandria, where the company was to perform that summer. While there, Warren rented an empty house and "hired" some furniture for his summer residence.[57] Shortly after his return to Baltimore, Cooper concluded his engagement, which resulted in

[54] *Ibid.*, February 17, April 8, 1807.
[55] Wood, *Personal Recollections*, 117.
[56] Baltimore *American*, May 5, 14, 1808.
[57] Warren, Journals, May 3, 1808.

a drastic drop in box-office receipts. In addition, Anne's preg-
nancy prevented her from performing after May 23. On that date
Warren afterward made the melancholy notation in his journal:
"the last night Mrs. W. ever performed."

Anne's condition undoubtedly prompted her husband to move
his family to Alexandria on June 3, one week before the end of
the spring season.[58] Although the doctors advised that her situation was "too critical to perform a journey, and to encounter its
attendant excitements," she ignored their advice, insisting on accompanying her husband in his summer management.[59] After
settling his family in Alexandria, Warren returned for the conclusion of the spring schedule, which ended with such low box-
office receipts that on June 10 he expressed his discouragement in
his journal: "the latter part of the season has faild—times are bad
—an Embargo—and all the Young Men are turning soldiers—we
all seem to be on the high Road to Ruin." On June 11 he left
Baltimore, arriving in time to dine the following day in Alexandria, where he found "all well" at his home.[60] But only a few days
later, Mrs. Warren "was seized with a violent illness . . . which
affected her brain, and deprived her of her senses during a part
of the time of her confinement. In her paroxysms, she would re-
cite passages from some of her favourite characters in such a
pathetic strain of declamation as would draw tears from all who
were witnesses of the sad spectacle."[61] However, on June 24, after
she delivered a stillborn son, she seemed considerably improved,
"having in some degree recovered her senses." Warren was sufficiently encouraged to look forward "to her ultimate recovery" and
attended rehearsals in high spirits on June 28, the day set for the
opening of the Alexandria theatre.[62] But at two in the afternoon
she suffered a relapse from which she never recovered. On that
day her grieving husband wrote: "On this day at 4 PM—My Be-

[58] Ibid., June 3, 1806.
[59] Durang, "The Philadelphia Stage," Chap. XLI, February 11, 1855.
[60] Warren, Journals, June 10, 12, 1808.
[61] "Confessions of a Rambler," Repository, V (London), February 1, 1825, pp.
101–105.
[62] Ibid., April 1, 1825, p. 226.

loved wife Ann expired—her sufferings have been great ever since the time of her delivery—now they are terminated—and we are left to mourn her loss—May God for ever bless her—she has not left a better woman behind—as to her talents as an actress—they are too well established to need any comment from me." Warren's grief was shared by many who also felt a personal and a professional loss. The news of her death "spread a general gloom—not only over the profession, but over the community—such was the esteem in which she was held by all. The stage lost an accomplished Lady and a most refined and talented actress."[63] Her obituary in a Philadelphia newspaper also expresses the sense of loss felt by others:

> Could the writer so command his feeling upon the present melancholy occasion, as to enable him to enter into a detail of the excellencies of Mrs. Warren's theatrical character, it would be superfluous, her celebrity having long since diffused itself over both her native and this her adopted country.
>
> In her the American stage has been deprived of its brightest ornament, not more conspicuous from her unrivalled excellence in her profession than from her having uniformly preserved a spotless and unsullied fame; proving by her example that an unblemished reputation is by no means incompatible with a theatrical life.
>
> In the circle of her intimate friends her loss will be most poignantly felt; for to them the many virtues and accomplishments which adorned her private life were best known. To a warm, feeling, and affectionate heart, were added that fascinating ease and grace in conversation, which, regulated by an excellent understanding, delighted, at the same time that it improved.
>
> But, alas! that eye is now dim and closed forever which has so often communicated its magic influence to the heart; and mute is that tongue whose flexible and silver tones so sympathetically vibrated upon the ear of an enraptured audience. And never could the observation of a celebrated moralist upon a similar occasion be more applicable than upon the present: "Death has eclipsed the gaiety of nations, and diminished the public of harmless pleasure."[64]

[63] Durang "The Philadelphia Stage," Chap. XLI, February 11, 1855.
[64] Philadelphia, *Gazette and Universal Daily Advertiser,* July 8, 1808.

Anne's burial in Christ Church yard, Alexandria, was attended
"by an immense assemblage of mourners."[65] A large cement vault
which marks her grave is still an object of interest to tourists who
continue to visit the small church, best known for its colonial
architecture and its famous pew-holders, George Washington and
Robert E. Lee. Few would realize as they read the inscription on
the actress' tomb that she enjoyed such distinction in her lifetime
that William Dunlap identified the year of her death, 1808, as
"remarkable in theatre history, wherever the English language is
spoken."[66] To most visitors today, the epitaph is no more than a
curious pause in the shady church yard, but undoubtedly to a
small but privileged generation of playgoers it would seem an altogether fitting and appropriate tribute:

Beneath this stone
are deposited
the remains of
Mrs. Anne Warren
Daughter of John Brunton Esq. of England
and wife of
William Warren Esq.
one of the managers of the Philadelphia
and Baltimore Theaters
By her loss
the American stage has been deprived of one of its
Brightest ornaments,
the unrivalled excellence of theatrical talents
was unsurpassed by the many virtues and
accomplishments which adorned her private life
In her were contained the affectionate wife
and mother and the sincere friend.
She died at Alexandria
June 28, 1808
aged 39 years

[65] "Confessions of a Rambler," February 1, 1825, p. 105.
[66] Dunlap, *History of the American Theatre*, II, 255.

VII

"The Most Perfect Actress America Has Seen"

". . . there was no similarity except in mind. Their persons and manners were indeed opposite, and . . . though Mrs. Merry made her way direct to the heart, the prize was won by gentleness. But Siddons seized upon it with a force that was irresistible."[1] William Dunlap thus compared the acting of Mrs. Merry to that of Mrs. Siddons. And John Bernard, who also saw them both said:

> Divided into two ranks as are the Shakespearean heroines, the queenly and the thoughtful, the loving and the passionate—if Mrs. Siddons, in the one ascended to a greatness that almost became an identity, Mrs. Merry on the other, I think was equally perfect, and equally gifted to enrapture an audience. With a voice that was all music, and a face all emotion, her pathos and tenderness were never exceeded; and if unequal to the grandeur of Katherine and Constance, her Juliet and Imogene were indelible images.[2]

These comparisons make obvious the roles most identified with Mrs. Merry. Throughout her career she was outstanding when performing characters of a loving, passionate but gentle nature, in contrast to the forceful masculine figures identified with Mrs. Siddons and her sister Mrs. Whitlock. Probably the role most suitable to Anne was Juliet, a part which she performed approximately fifty-seven times, more than any other during her career. At the age of sixteen, when she first appeared as Juliet she was ideally suited to the role in age and appearance. Endowed with a graceful body and a melodious voice, she gave life to the early

[1] Dunlap, *History of the American Theatre*, I, 337.
[2] Bernard, *Retrospections of America*, 268–69.

140

scenes of the tragedy depicting youthful innocence and young passionate love. Until she expanded her emotional range through a wider knowledge of life, providing insight into the emotional depths of the role, she probably relied upon the energy of her voice and spirited deportment in the more demanding scenes. As she matured as a person and an artist, she found new dimensions for the role. She maintained the delicacy and simplicity of the youthful Juliet and at the same time gave the later scenes pathos, strength, and energy without suggesting masculine coarseness. The combination of these talents led Dunlap to declare that Mrs. Merry's was "perhaps the best representation of Juliet that was ever seen or heard."[3] Other comparable Shakespearean heroines indelibly stamped with Mrs. Merry's excellence were Desdemona, Cordelia, Lady Ann, Perdita, and Ophelia. But noticeably she did not play the "queenly and thoughtful" types such as Lady Macbeth and Katherine.

Because she could portray the gentle, loving, and passionate tragic figures, she was well suited to give life to the tender, feminine heroines of sentimental comedy and melodrama whose loving, patient natures helped them endure and triumph over hardship and deprivation: Julia, Indiana, Amanthis, Louisa Courtney, Sophia, Cora, Angela, Mrs. Haller, and Emily Tempest. She could also portray such comic heroines as Lady Teazle and Beatrice but she avoided the hoyden types so ably played by Mrs. Jordan and Mrs. Marshall. Although she became most identified with tragic roles, she devoted a substantial part of her repertoire to her pathetic and melodramatic heroines, making her an exceptional asset to the Chestnut Street company.

To know Mrs. Merry's roles provides insight into the quality of her acting; yet a more precise description of her particular physical endowments leads to a fuller appreciation of her artistry. During her English career she was often described as "under size," but in America, of "middle size." Regardless of this difference, the shortness of her figure may have been a disadvantage in suggesting a majestic appearance. But it was a handicap dismissed during her

[3] Dunlap, *History of the American Theatre*, I, 308.

later career, for it was rarely mentioned by American critics. No doubt one of her most outstanding attributes was a graceful body. Through her gracefulness Mrs. Merry pleased turn-of-the-century theatergoers whose ideal was changing from the neo-Classic to the Romantic. She made her movement appear "natural" as well as appropriate. She was able to depict a dignified body attitude while simultaneously suggesting the naturalness of a "child of nature." Although the term "natural" is variously defined, in this case it can perhaps best be understood in relation to another critical term often associated with Mrs. Merry's acting, "chaste." In the eighteenth century "chaste" was employed to describe subdued and simple acting devoid of premeditated affects.[4] A chaste actor avoided tricks of voice or movement designed to manipulate an audience into spontaneous applause; instead, he attempted to reveal the imagined character by subordinating the actor to the role with no attention to external side-effects. (In twentieth century terms, chaste acting might be described as honest character portrayal, free of self-indulgences designed to display the actor's virtuosity rather than the character.) Chaste acting was a complimentary description bestowed upon Macklin, Henderson, and Mrs. Siddons, all of whom Mrs. Merry had an opportunity to observe. And throughout her career, she received the same accolade.

Probably Anne's most distinguishing attribute was her voice, "the most melodious we ever heard," as it was once described. "Beautifully feminine," with "rare sweetness," and clarity, its basic quality particularly suited the gentle, loving heroines which dominated her repertoire. In addition her voice was flexible and expressive, capable of revealing varieties of emotions and nuances of feeling. Within the compass of a single sentence she could convey "grief, shame and despair." Another skill for which she frequently earned admiration was her accurate line readings, resulting from correct word emphasis and vocal inflection. Although she was occasionally criticized for excessive or erroneous empha-

---

4 Joseph, *The Tragic Actor*, 238.

sis, usually, in her placement of emphasis she was called "remarkably correct and impressive."

Mrs. Merry was never described as beautiful. At best her features were labeled "agreeable." But if her face lacked beauty, she was endowed with an expressive countenance marked by "feminine sweetness" and the ability to express the passions with energy and force. This use of her face was apparently a skill acquired through her own perseverance. The English critic Joseph Haslewood said that her features were "neither delicate nor expressive";[5] yet, within the years immediately following her debut, her "mobile face," "vivacious countenance," "expressive eyes," and "tenderness of look" became distinguishing aspects of her performances. In addition, through her "expressive listening," she revealed the inner life of a character, often anticipating speeches and movement. Mrs. Merry's attributes and techniques—"eloquent pauses," "expressive countenance," "thrilling tones," and "graceful motion"— combined so remarkably that she won acclaim for her ability to stir listeners. Witnesses to her acting were often hushed to awed silence or moved to "abundant tears."

Although her American career spanned only twelve years, she had considerable influence and impact upon the American theatre. Arriving at the Chestnut Street theatre at the age of twenty-seven, she won acclaim as the "most perfect actress America has seen";[6] the fact that she was undoubtedly the only actress in the United States with such extensive experience in leading roles on a great London stage supports belief in her genuine superiority. She had also come at a personally propitious moment to test the full range of her artistic powers on the great roles of the contemporary repertoire. If the challenge was physically gruelling, with her unusual talent she thrived and prospered, commanding the most famous roles of her day. As the country's foremost actress, Mrs. Merry developed new standards consistently higher than those of any other performer. On the other hand, although

[5] Haslewood, *The Secret History of the Green-Room*, II, 88.
[6] Dunlap, *History of the American Theatre*, I, 334.

James Fennell's genius was acknowledged, he was so erratic that he could not set a permanent standard.

Not limited to acting, Mrs. Merry extended her influence to management. Although she served as director for only two years, during that time she set the high standards of her own art for the company as a whole, insisting on a well-regulated, carefully executed theatre operation. But whether she was performing as leading actress or manager, or both, Mrs. Merry influenced the entire company through her own personal qualities, leaving her impact on her associates, on her profession, and on the American theatre as an institution; for just as she was greatly admired as an artist, so, also, she was equally respected for her own personal character. In her private life she stood out in contrast to other theatre people to such an extent that she drew commendation as early as her second year in London. Because of her good name, Anne Merry was invited into some of the most prominent homes in Philadelphia and travelled in a social sphere previously closed to actors. As her obituary testifies, her "spotless and unsullied Fame" did much to convince the early American public that "an unblemished reputation is by no means incompatible with theatrical life." Consequently in just those twelve years, she helped win for acting a new level of social acceptance.

As is characteristic with most performing artists, Mrs. Merry exercised the greatest impact while she was alive. In spite of her brilliance she remains a relatively unknown artist. Because fame is often as much a matter of time and place as of intrinsic merit, part of the reason for her obscurity is that during the height of her artistic powers she was not associated with a major theatrical center; although the Chestnut Street theatre was the foremost in the young country, it lacked the renown and prestige of the world-famous playhouses which might have brought her more lasting recognition. Moreover Mrs. Merry's preëminence remains unrecognized because of the lack of an adequate yardstick by which to measure her ability. Performing at Covent Garden, during the same years in which Mrs. Siddons was playing at Drury Lane, Mrs. Merry was too young and inexperienced to gain a valid comparison with the great actress. And by the time she had developed adequately to meet a substantial challenge, Mrs. Merry moved to the United States, where she never encountered really significant competition. Thus, Anne Brunton Merry's place in the long view of theatre history remains difficult to assess, although she fulfilled the promise of her "early excellence" as she became the finest actress in America during her lifetime.

Appendix:
Roles Played by
Anne Brunton Merry

The following is a chronological list of the roles known to have been performed by Anne Brunton Merry, with the name of the author, and the translator or adaptor, when appropriate, and the date and name of the city of the first performance. The list has been drawn from the works of Genest, Clark, Pollock, from British and American newspapers, and from William Warren's journal.

1. Euphrasia in *The Grecian Daughter* by Arthur Murphy, February, 1785, Bristol.

2. Horatia in *The Roman Father*, adapted by William Whitehead from Corneille's *Horace*, May 3, 1785, Bath.

3. Palmira in *Mahomet*, adapted by James Miller from Voltaire's *Mahomet*, May 24, 1785, Bath.

4. Juliet in *Romeo and Juliet* by William Shakespeare, November 14, 1785, London.

5. Monimia in *The Orphan* by Thomas Otway, December 1, 1785, London.

6. Hermione in *The Distressed Mother*, translated by Ambrose Philips from Racine's *Andromaque*, January 31, 1786, London.

7. Athanais in *Theodosius* by Nathaniel Lee, February 23, 1786, London.

8. Cordelia in *King Lear* by William Shakespeare, March 6, 1786, London.

9. Charlotte in *Werter*, adapted by Frederick Reynolds from Goethe's novella, March 14, 1786, London.

10. Fidelia in *The Foundling* by Edward Moore, April 8, 1786, London.

11. Zara in *The Mourning Bride* by William Congreve, April 19, 1786, London.

12. Alicia in *The Tragedy of Jane Shore* by Nicholas Rowe, October 6, 1786, London.

13. Calista in *The Fair Penitent* by Nicholas Rowe, November 27, 1786, London.

14. Eloisa in *Eloisa* by Frederick Reynolds, December 23, 1786, London.

15. Beatrice in *Much Ado About Nothing* by William Shakespeare, April 11, 1787, London.

16. Harriet in *The Guardian* by David Garrick, April 11, 1787, London.

17. Cecelia in *Chapter of Accidents* by Sophia Lee, April 17, 1787, London.

18. Perdita in *The Winter's Tale* by William Shakespeare, May 21, 1787, London.

19. Statira in *Alexander The Great* by Nathaniel Lee, October 22, 1787, London.

20. Louisa in *All on a Summer's Day* by Elizabeth Inchbald, December 15, 1787, London.

21. Panthea in *King and No King* by Beaumont and Fletcher, January 14, 1788, London.

22. Indiana in *The Conscious Lovers* by Sir Richard Steele, February 4, 1788, London.

23. Almeria in *The Mourning Bride* by William Congreve, March 10, 1788, London.

24. Julia in *The Rivals* by Richard B. Sheridan, March 28, 1788, London.

25. Lady Clairville in *Ton or the Follies of Fashion* by Lady Wallace, April 8, 1788, London.

26. Harriett in *The Jealous Wife* by George Colman, April 23, 1788, London.

27. Leonora in *The Revenge* by Edward Young, October 3, 1788, London.

28. Amanthis in *The Child of Nature*, adapted from the French by Elizabeth Inchbald, October 28, 1788, London.

29. Lady Jane in *The Toy or Hampton Court Frolics* by John O'Keeffe, February 3, 1789, London.

30. Miss Richland in *The Good-Natured Man* by Oliver Goldsmith, April 20, 1789, London.

31. Lady Charlot in *The Funeral* by Sir Richard Steele, April 30, 1789, London.

32. Louisa Courtney in *The Dramatist* by Frederick Reynolds, May 15, 1789, London.

33. Arabella in *More Ways Than One* by Hannah Cowley, May 19, 1789, London.

34. Lady Anne in *Richard III* by William Shakespeare, September 25, 1789, London.

35. Fanny in *The Clandestine Marriage* by David Garrick and George Colman (the Elder), November 27, 1789, London.

36. Mrs. Strictland in *The Suspicious Husband* by Benjamin Hoadley, December 31, 1789, London.

37. Penelope in *The Gamester* by James Shirley, altered by David Garrick, January 22, 1790, London.

38. Adelaide in *The Count of Narbonne* by Robert Jephson, March 22, 1790, London.

39. Indamora in *The Widow of Malabar* by Mariana Starke, May 5, 1790, London.

40. Cleopatra in *All For Love* by John Dryden, May 24, 1790, London.

41. Angelina in *Love Makes a Man* by Colley Cibber, December 10, 1790, London.

42. Louisa in *The Picture of Paris* by Robert Merry, December 21, 1790, London.

43. Lydia in *School For Arrogance* by Thomas Holcroft, February 4, 1791, London.

44. Zoriana in *Lorenzo* by Robert Merry, April 5, 1791, London.

45. Countess of Rutland in *Earl of Essex* by Henry Jones, April 11, 1791, London.

46. Sylvia in *The Double Gallant* by Colley Cibber, May 11, 1791, London.

47. Lady Amaranth in *Wild Oats* by John O'Keeffe, December 15, 1791, London.

48. Sigismunda in *Tancred and Sigismunda* by James Thompson, December 21, 1791, London.

49. Sophia in *The Road to Ruin* by Thomas Holcroft, February 18, 1792, London.

50. Emily Tempest in *The Wheel of Fortune* by Richard Cumberland, December 30, 1796, Philadelphia.

51. Marchioness Merida in *The Child of Nature*, January 9, 1797, Philadelphia.

52. Donna Violante in *The Wonder: A Woman Keeps a Secret* by Susanna Centlivre, January 11, 1797, Philadelphia.

53. Lady Eleanor Irwin in *Every One Has His Fault* by Elizabeth Inchbald, January 18, 1797, Philadelphia.

54. Belvidera in *Venice Preserv'd* by Thomas Otway, January 21, 1797, Philadelphia.

55. Cora in *Columbus* by Thomas Morton, January 30, 1797, Philadelphia.

56. Julia Faulkner in *The Way to Get Married* by Thomas Morton, February 13, 1797, Philadelphia.

57. Julia in *The Abbey of St. Augustine* by Robert Merry, March 20, 1797, Philadelphia.

58. Portia in *The Merchant of Venice* by William Shakespeare, March 27, 1797, Philadelphia.

59. Zeraphine in *The Ransomed Slave* by Robert Merry, March 29, 1797, Philadelphia.

60. Gertrude in *Hamlet* by William Shakespeare, March 31, 1797, Philadelphia.

61. Paulina in *Love's Frailties* by Thomas Holcroft, April 5, 1797, Philadelphia.

62. Helen in *The Iron Chest* by George Colman, Jr., April 17, 1797, Philadelphia.

63. Charlotte in *Heigh Ho! for a Husband* by Frances Waldron, April 24, 1797, Philadelphia.

64. Clarinthia in *An Ancient Day* by Sam Relf, May 3, 1797, Philadelphia.

65. Desdemona in *Othello* by William Shakespeare, September 29, 1797, New York.

66. Miss Dorillon in *Wives as They Were and Maids as They Are* by Elizabeth Inchbald, October 13, 1797, New York.

67. Roxana in *Alexander the Great* by Nathaniel Lee, November 24, 1797, New York.

68. Isabella in *Isabella* by Thomas Southerne, January 19, 1798, Philadelphia.

69. Eloisa in *Fenelon* by Robert Merry, February 2, 1798, Philadelphia.

70. Mrs. Beverly in *The Gamester* by Edward Moore, February 15, 1798, Philadelphia.

71. Lady Teazle in *The School for Scandal* by Richard B. Sheridan, March 21, 1798, Philadelphia.

72. Cowslip in *The Agreeable Surprize* by John O'Keeffe, March 21, 1798, Philadelphia.

73. Charlotte in *He Would Be A Soldier* by Frederick Pilon, March 26, 1798, Philadelphia.

74. Louisa in *The Prodigal* by Francis Waldron, March 28, 1798, Philadelphia.

75. Ellena in *The Italian Monk* by James Boaden, April 11, 1798, Philadelphia.

76. Lady Ann in *The Deserted Daughter* by Thomas Holcroft, April 13, 1798, Philadelphia.

77. Agnes in *The Fatal Curiosity* by George Lillo, April 18, 1798, Philadelphia.

78. Elvina in *The Spectre, or The Castle of the Forest*, April 23, 1798, Philadelphia.

79. Charlotte in *The Fatal Curiosity* by George Lillo, November 29, 1798, Baltimore.

80. Mrs. Greville in *Secrets Worth Knowing* by Thomas Morton, December 19, 1798, Baltimore.

81. Cicely Homespun in *The Heir at Law* by George Colman, Jr., February 13, 1799, Philadelphia.

82. Elinor Bromly in *Cheap Living* by Frederick Reynolds, February 25, 1799, Philadelphia.

83. Clara Forrester in *Duplicity* by Thomas Holcroft, March 6, 1799, Philadelphia.

84. Maria in *A Wedding in Wales* by Dr. Stock, March 11, 1799, Philadelphia.

85. Mrs. Haller in *The Stranger* by William Dunlap, from the German of Kotzebue, April 1, 1799, Philadelphia.

86. Lady Jane in *He's Much to Blame* by Thomas Holcroft, April 3, 1799, Philadelphia.

87. Countess Rosela in *The Mysterious Marriage* by Harriet Lee, April 5, 1799, Philadelphia.

88. Juliana in *False and True* by Reverend Moultru, April 13, 1799, Philadelphia.

89. Julia in *The Mysteries of the Castle* by Miles Peter Andrews, April 15, 1799, Philadelphia.

90. Lady Terrendal in *Life's Vagaries or Innocence Protected* by John O'Keeffe, April 17, 1799, Philadelphia.

91. Eleonora in *Edward and Eleonora* by James Thomson, April 24, 1799, Philadelphia.

92. Amelia in *The Robbers*, taken from Schiller, April 26, 1799, Philadelphia.

93. Emily Fitzallan in *False Impressions* by Richard Cumberland, May 1, 1799, Philadelphia.

94. Agatha in *Lovers' Vows* by Elizabeth Inchbald, from the German of Kotzebue, May 24, 1799, Philadelphia.

95. Lady Paragon in *The Natural Son* by Richard Cumberland, October 11, 1799, Baltimore.

96. Rosa in *The Secret* by Edward Morris, December 30, 1799, Philadelphia.

97. Emma in *The Reconciliation or The Birth-Day*, translated by Thomas Dibdin from the German of Kotzebue, January 20, 1800, Philadelphia.

98. Elizabeth von Hailwyl in *The Count of Burgundy*, by Plumptre from the German of Kotzebue, February 19, 1800, Philadelphia.

99. Orellana in *Peru Aveng'd* by Arthur Murphy, March 2, 1800, Philadelphia.

100. Jane in *The Tragedy of Jane Shore* by Nicholas Rowe, March 11, 1800, Philadelphia.

101. Angela in *The Castle Spectre* by M. G. Lewis, April 2, 1800, Philadelphia.

102. Amelia in *False Shame*, translated by William Dunlap from the German of Kotzebue, April 14, 1800, Philadelphia.

103. Yarico in *Inkle and Yarico* by George Colman, Jr., April 14, 1800, Philadelphia.

104. Josephine in *Sighs; or The Daughter* by Prince Hoare, from the German of Kotzebue, April 16, 1800, Philadelphia.

105. Mrs. Mortimer in *Laugh When You Can* by Frederick Reynolds, April 18, 1800, Philadelphia.

106. Lady Percy in *Henry IV* by William Shakespeare, April 19, 1800, Philadelphia.

107. Constance in *King John* by William Shakespeare, April 21, 1800, Philadelphia.

108. Ophelia in *Hamlet* by William Shakespeare, April 26, 1800, Philadelphia.

109. Clarinda in *The Suspicious Husband* by John Hoadly, April 28, 1800, Philadelphia.

110. Elvira in *Pizarro,* adapted from the German of Kotzebue by Richard B. Sheridan, May 14, 1800, Philadelphia.

111. Juliana in *Management* by Frederick Reynolds, October 27, 1800, Philadelphia.

112. Sophia in *The Law of Lombardy* by Robert Jephson, November 24, 1800, Philadelphia.

113. Zorayda in *The East Indian* by M. G. Lewis, December 18, 1800, Philadelphia.

114. Elgiva in *Edwy and Elgiva* by Charles Jared Ingersoll, April 4, 1801, Philadelphia.

115. Cora in *Virgin of the Sun* by Benjamin Thompson, from the German of Kotzebue, February 12, 1802, Philadelphia.

116. Eloisa in *Joanna of Montfaucon,* translated by Richard Cumberland, from the German of Kotzebue, February 12, 1802, Philadelphia.

117. Bertha in *Point of Honour* taken from the French by Charles Kemble, February 22, 1802, Philadelphia.

118. Lady Melmoth in *Folly as it Flies* by Frederick Reynolds, February 26, 1802, Philadelphia.

119. Cara Bonito in *The Blind Girl* by Thomas Morton, March 10, 1802, Philadelphia.

120. Innogen in *Adelmorn* by M. G. Lewis, April 12, 1802, Philadelphia.

121. Rosamunda in *Abaellino, The Great Bandit*, translated by William Dunlap from the German of Johan Zschokke, January 12, 1803, Baltimore.

122. Amelrosa in *Alfonso, King of Castile* by M. G. Lewis, May 16, 1803, Baltimore.

123. Lilla in *The Voice of Nature*, adapted by William Dunlap from *Le Jugement de Salomon* by L. C. Caigniez, June 10, 1803, Baltimore.

124. Mrs. Ford in *Merry Wives of Windsor* by William Shakespeare, January 25, 1804, Philadelphia.

125. Stella in *Maid of Bristol* by James Boaden, February 13, 1804, Philadelphia.

126. Eliza in *Hear Both Sides* by Thomas Holcroft, February 27, 1804, Philadelphia.

127. Christina in *Gustavus Vasa* by Henry Brooke, March 13, 1804, Philadelphia.

128. Sophia Dove in *The Brothers; or, The Fortunate Shipwreck* by Richard Cumberland, March 26, 1804, Philadelphia.

129. Louisa in *The Sailor's Daughter* by Richard Cumberland, November 14, 1804, Baltimore.

130. Countess Belfior in *The Wife of Two Husbands*, adapted by James Cobb from the French of Guilbert Pixérecourt, November 22, 1804, Baltimore.

131. Suzette in *Guilty or Not Guilty* by Thomas Dibdin, November 26, 1804, Baltimore.

132. Umba in *La Perouse; or The Deserted Island*, translated by William Dunlap from the German of Kotzebue, December 26, 1804, Philadelphia.

133. Lady Macbeth in *Macbeth* by William Shakespeare, January 16, 1805, Philadelphia.

134. Cleone in *Cleone* by Robert Dodsley, February 20, 1805, Philadelphia.

135. Daughter to Scander in *Selima and Azor*, Persian tale from the
French by Richard B. Sheridan, March 6, 1805, Philadelphia.

136. Roxalana in *The Sultan* by Isaac Bickerstaff, March 11, 1805,
Philadelphia.

137. Young Lady in *I'll Tell You What* by Elizabeth Inchbald, March
15, 1805, Philadelphia.

138. Mary in *Mary, Queen of Scots* by St. John, November 28, 1805,
Baltimore.

139. Juliana in *The Honey Moon* by John Tobin, February 24, 1806,
Philadelphia.

140. Mrs. Villars in *The Blind Bargain* by Frederick Reynolds, February 26, 1806, Philadelphia.

141. Seraphina in *Lewis of Monte Blanco* by William Dunlap, March
10, 1806, Philadelphia.

142. Estrifania in *Rule a Wife and Have a Wife* by Beaumont and
Fletcher, March 26, 1806, Philadelphia.

143. Clarissa in *Lionel and Clarissa* by Isaac Bickerstaff, May 19,
1806, Philadelphia.

144. Lady Transit in *A Hint to Husbands* by Richard Cumberland,
October 31, 1806, Baltimore.

145. Mrs. Hamilton in *School for Friends* by Miss Chambers, November 24, 1806, Baltimore.

146. Lady Townly in *The Provok'd Husband* by Colley Cibber,
March 20, 1807, Philadelphia.

147. Marchioness Merida in *The Travellers* by A. Cherry, April 20,
1807, Baltimore.

148. Madame Clermont in *Adrian and Orilla* by William Dimond,
February 12, 1808, Philadelphia.

149. Olivia Wyndham in *Time's a Tell-Tale* by Henry Siddons, March 4, 1808, Philadelphia.

150. Laetitia Hardy in *The Belle's Stratagem* by Hannah Cowley, March 7, 1808, Philadelphia.

Bibliography

BOOKS

Adams, M. Ray. *Studies in the Literary Background of English Radicalism*. Lancaster, 1947.

Baker, David Erskine. *Biographia Dramatica*. London, 1812.

Balderson, Katherine C., ed. *Thraliana. The Diary of Mrs. Hester Lynch Thrale (later Mrs. Piozzi) 1776–1809*. 2 vols. Oxford, 1951.

Barrett, Charlotte, ed. *Diary and Letters of Madame D'Arblay, July, 1791–April, 1802*. 6 vols. New York, 1904–1905.

Bernard, John. *Retrospections of America, 1797–1811*, ed. Laurence Hutton and Brander Matthews. New York, 1887.

———. *Retrospections of the Stage, 1756–1787*. 2 vols. Boston, 1832.

Bernbaum, Ernest. *The Drama of Sensibility: A Sketch of the History of Sentimental Comedy and Domestic Tragedy, 1696–1780*. Boston, 1915.

Boaden, James. *Memoirs of the Life of John Philip Kemble, Esq., including a History of the Stage, from the Time of Garrick to the Present Period*. 2 vols. London, 1825.

Board, M. E. *The Story of the Bristol Stage, 1490–1925*. London, 1925.

Boas, Frederick S. *An Introduction to Eighteenth Century Drama, 1700–1780*. New York, 1953.

Brayley, Edward Wedlake. *Historical Accounts of the Theatres of London*. London, 1826.

Brigham, Clarence S. *History and Bibliography of American Newspapers, 1690–1820; including Additions and Corrections, 1961*. Hamden, Conn., 1962.

The British Album. Boston, 1793.

Brown, T. Allston. *History of the American Stage*. New York, 1870.

———. *History of the New York Stage . . . 1733 to 1870*. New York, 1903.

Campbell, Thomas. *Life of Mrs. Siddons*. London, 1839.

Clapp, William Warland. *A Record of the Boston Stage*. Boston, 1853.

Clark, Roy Benjamin. *William Gifford: Tory Satirist, Critic, and Editor*. New York, 1930.

Clark, William Smith. *The Irish Stage in the County Towns, 1720 to 1800*. Oxford, 1965

Clayden, P. W. *The Early Life of Samuel Rogers*. London, 1887.

Clifford, James L. *Hester Lynch Piozzi (Mrs. Thrale)*. Oxford, 1941.

Coad, Oral Sumner and Edwin Mims, Jr. "The American Stage" in *The Pageant of America*, XIV. New Haven, 1929.

Davies, Thomas. *A Genuine Narrative of the Life and Theatrical Transactions of Mr. John Henderson*. London, 1777.

Davis, Deering, Stephen Dorsey, and Ralph Hall. *Georgetown Houses of the Federal Period, 1780–1830*. Cornwall, N. Y., 1944.

Dobrée, Bonamy. *Restoration Tragedy, 1660–1720*. Oxford, 1929.

Dunlap, William. *Diary of William Dunlap*. 3 vols. New York, 1930.

————. *History of the American Theatre*. 2 vols. London, 1833.

Durang, John. *The Memoir of John Durang: American Actor, 1785–1816*, ed., Alan S. Downer. Pittsburgh, 1966.

Fennell, James. *An Apology for the Life of James Fennell*. Philadelphia, 1814.

The Florence Miscellany. Florence, 1785.

Genest, John. *Some Account of the English Stage*. 10 vols. Bath, 1832.

Gifford, William. *The Baviad and Maeviad*. Philadelphia, 1799.

Gilliland, Thomas. *The Dramatic Mirror*. 2 vols. London, 1808.

Gray, Charles H. *Theatrical Criticism in London to 1795*. New York, 1931.

Graydon, Alexander. *Memoirs of a Life Chiefly Passed in Pennsylvania within the Last Sixty Years*. Harrisburg, 1811.

Hamer, Philip M. *A Guide to Archives and Manuscripts in the United States*. New Haven, 1961.

Haslewood, Joseph. *The Secret History of the Green-Room*. 2 vols. London, 1795.

Hitchcock, Robert. *An Historical View of the Irish Stage From the Earliest Period Down to the Close of the Season of 1788*. Dublin, 1788.

Hogan, Charles Beecher, ed. *The London Stage*. Vol. 5. Pt. 2. Carbondale, 1968.

Holcroft, Thomas. *Memoirs of Thomas Holcroft Written by Himself and Continued by William Hazlitt*. London, 1816.

Hornblow, Arthur. *A History of the Theatre in America From Its Beginning to the Present Time*. Philadelphia, 1919.

Ireland, Joseph Norton. *A Memoir of the Professional Life of Thomas Abthorpe Cooper*. New York, 1888.

————. *Records of the New York Stage from 1750 to 1860*. 2 vols. New York, 1866.

Jackson, Joseph. *The Encyclopedia of Philadelphia*. 4 vols. Harrisburg, 1931–33.

James, Reese Davis. *Cradle of Culture: The Philadelphia Stage, 1800–1810*. Philadelphia, 1957.

————. *Old Drury of Philadelphia, A History of the Philadelphia Stage 1800–1835*. Philadelphia, 1932.

Joseph, Bertram. *The Tragic Actor*. London, 1959.

Kavanagh, Peter. *The Irish Theatre: Being a History of the Drama in Ireland from the Earliest Period up to the Present Day*. Tralee, Ireland, 1946.

Loftis, John C. *Essays on the Theatre from Eighteenth Century Periodicals*. London, 1950.

Longaker, J. M. *The Della Cruscans and William Gifford*. Philadelphia, 1924.

Macmillan, Dougald (comp.). *Catalogue of the Larpent Plays in the Huntington Library*. San Marino, 1939.

McNamara, Brooks, *The American Playhouse in the Eighteenth Century* (Cambridge, 1969).

Marshall, Roderick R. *Italy in English Literature, 1755–1815*. New York, 1934.

Mease, James. *The Picture of Philadelphia*. Philadelphia, 1811.

Morison, Stanley. *The English Newspaper*. Cambridge, 1932.

Nicoll, Allardyce. *A History of Early Nineteenth Century Drama 1800–1850*. Cambridge, 1925.

————. *A History of Early Eighteenth Century Drama 1700–1750*. Cambridge, 1925.

————. *A History of Late Eighteenth Century Drama 1750–1800*. Cambridge, 1927.

Nye, Russel Blaine. *The Cultural Life of the New Nation 1776–1800.* New York, 1960.

Oberholtzer, Ellis Paxson. *Philadelphia: A History of the City and Its People.* 2 vols. Philadelphia, 1912.

Odell, George C. D. *Annals of the New York Stage.* 15 vols. New York, 1927–1949.

O'Keeffe, John. *Recollections of the Life of John O'Keeffe written by Himself.* 2 vols. London, 1826.

Oulton, Walley Chamberlain. *The History of the Theatres of London: Containing An Annual Register Of All The New and Revived Tragedies, Comedies, Operas, Farces, Pantomime and C. That Have Been Performed at the Theatres Royal, In London, From the Year 1771 to 1795.* 2 vols. London, 1796.

Paul, Charles Kegan. *William Godwin, His Friends and Contemporaries.* Boston, 1876.

Penley, Belville S. *The Bath Stage.* London, 1892.

Plumb, J. H. *England in the Eighteenth Century.* Baltimore, 1950.

Pollock, Thomas Clark. *The Philadelphia Stage in the Eighteenth Century.* Philadelphia, 1933.

Powell, Mary G. *The History of Old Alexandria, Virginia.* Richmond, 1928.

Quinn, Arthur Hobson. *A History of the American Drama, from the Beginning to the Civil War.* New York, 1923.

Reynolds, Frederick. *The Life and Times of Frederick Reynolds written by Himself.* 2 vols. London, 1827.

St. Méry, Moreau de. *American Journey, 1793–1797.* Kenneth Roberts and Anna M. Roberts, ed. and trans. New York, 1947.

Scharf, J. Thomas, and Thompson Westcott. *A History of Philadelphia, 1609–1884.* 3 vols. Philadelphia, 1884.

Seilhamer, G. O. *History of the American Theatre.* 3 vols. Philadelphia, 1888–1891.

Shawe-Taylor, Desmond. *Covent Garden.* New York, 1948.

Southern, Richard. *The Georgian Playhouse.* London, 1948.

Smyth, Albert H. *The Philadelphia Magazines and Their Contributors 1741–1850.* Philadelphia, 1892.

Stockwell, La Tourette. *Dublin Theatres and Theatre Customs 1637–1820.* Appleton, 1938.

Tatum, George B. *Penn's Great Town: 250 Years of Philadelphia Architecture.* Philadelphia, 1961.

Taylor, John. *Records of My Life.* 2 vols. London, 1832.

The Thespian Dictionary. London, 1802.

Watson, John F. *Annuals of Philadelphia and Pennsylvania in the Older Time.* Philadelphia, 1850.

Wood, William B. *Personal Recollections of the Stage.* Philadelphia, 1855.

Wyndham, Henry Saxe. *The Annals of Covent Garden Theatre from 1732 to 1897.* 2 vols. London, 1906.

PERIODICALS

Adams, M. Ray. "Della Cruscanism in America," *PMLA*, LXXIX (June, 1964), 259–65.

———. "A Newly Discovered Play of Robert Merry Written in America," *Manuscripts*, XIII (Fall, 1961), 20–26.

———. "Robert Merry and the American Theatre," *Theatre Survey*, VI (May, 1965), 1–9.

———. "Robert Merry, Political Romanticist," *Studies in Romanticism*, II (Fall, 1962), 23–27.

"Biographical Sketch of Mrs. Warren," *The Mirror of Taste and Dramatic Censor*, I (February, 1810), 118–33.

Bostetter, Edward E. "The Original Della Cruscans and the *Florence Miscellany*," *Huntington Library Quarterly*, XIX (May, 1956), 277–300.

Clifford, James L. "Robert Merry—a Pre-Byronic Hero," *Bulletin of the John Rylands Library*, XXVII (1942–43), 74–96.

Condie, Thomas. "'Biographical Anecdotes of Mrs. Merry of the Theatre, Philadelphia," *The Philadelphia Monthly Magazine, or Universal Repository of Knowledge and Entertainment*, I (April, 1798), 185–88.

"Confessions of a Rambler," *The Repository* (London), V (February, April, 1825), 101–105, 226.

"Description of the New Theatre," *The New York Magazine; or, Literary Repository*, (April, 1794), 195.

"Diary of Mrs. William Thornton, 1800–1863," *Records of the Columbia Historical Society*, X (1907), 88–226.

Dorland, W. A. Newman. "The Second Troop Philadelphia City Cavalry," *Pennsylvania Magazine of History and Biography*, XLVI (1922), 262–71.

NEWSPAPERS

Alexandria *The Columbian Mirror and Alexandria Gazette.*
Baltimore *American and Commercial Daily Advertiser.*
Baltimore *Federal Gazette and Baltimore Daily Advertiser.*
Georgetown *The Centinel of Liberty and George-Town and Washington Advertiser.*
London *The Daily Universal Register.*
London *The Times.*
New York *Commercial Advertiser.*
New York *Evening Post.*
Philadelphia *Aurora General Advertiser.*
Philadelphia *Gazette and Universal Daily Advertiser.*
Philadelphia *Gazette of the United States and Philadelphia Daily Advertiser.*
Philadelphia *Porcupine's Gazette.*
Philadelphia *Poulson's American Daily Advertiser.*

OTHER PERIODICALS CONSULTED

European Magazine (London)
Gentlemen's Magazine (London)
Monthly Magazine and British Register (London)
Philadelphia Monthly Magazine (Philadelphia)
Port Folio (Philadelphia)
The Repository (London)
Theatrical Censor (Philadelphia)
Theatrical Censor and Critical Miscellany (Philadelphia)

UNPUBLISHED MATERIALS

Letters

Copy of a letter from Anne Wignell to Mrs. Thackerson, Baltimore, October 4, 1804. The location of the original is not known. The copy is in the Alexandria Public Library, Alexandria, Virginia.

Manuscripts and Scrapbooks

Durang, Charles. "The Philadelphia Stage, from the Year 1749 to the Year 1855. Partly Compiled from the Papers of His Father, the Late John Durang, with Notes by the Editors [of the Philadelphia *Sunday Dispatch*]." May 7, 1854 to July 8, 1860. The complete file is in six bound volumes in the library of the University of Pennsylvania.

May, Alonso J. "Dramatic Encyclopedia of Baltimore, 1750–1904." This uncompleted manuscript is available at the Maryland Historical Society, Baltimore.

Warren, Anna. Scrapbook. Channing Pollock Theatre Collection, Howard University, Washington, D. C.

Warren, William I. Journals, 1796–1831. Channing Pollock Theatre Collection, Howard University, Washington, D. C.

Theses and Dissertations

Greenfield, Mildred Albert. "The Early History of the Theatre in Baltimore." M.A. thesis, Johns Hopkins University, 1953.

Harbin, Billy J. "The Career of John Hodgkinson in the American Theatre." Ph.D. dissertation, Indiana University, 1970.

McKenzie, Ruth Harsha. "Organization, Production and Management of the Chestnut Street Theatre, Philadelphia, from 1791–1820." Ph.D. dissertation, Stanford University, 1952.

Michael, Mary Ruth. "A History of the Professional Theatre in Boston From the Beginning to 1816." Ph.D. dissertation, Radcliffe College, 1941.

Pritner, Calvin Lee. "William Warren's Management of the Chestnut Street Theatre Company." Ph.D. dissertation, University of Illinois, 1964.

Stine, Richard. "The Philadelphia Theatre, 1682–1829: Its Growth as a Cultural Institution." Ph.D. dissertation, University of Pennsylvania, 1951.

Index

Accademia della Crusca, 36
Achmet, Catherine Ann, 31
Anderson, Samuel, 68, 69

Bannister, Charles, 19
Baviad, The, 44
Benson, Peter, 109n, 128n
Benson, Peter, Mrs. *See* Wignell, Elizabeth
Bernard, John, 7, 9, 38, 60, 61, 64, 66, 68, 70, 71, 75, 84, 99, 109, 135, 140
Blissett, Francis, 80, 105, 114, 124
British Album, The, 37
Brunton, Anne; at Alexandria, 76, 137, 139; at Annapolis, 67, 68, 69, 71, 75, 120; at Baltimore, 58–59, 67, 70–71, 74, 76, 79 86, 103, 108, 114, 115, 119, 121–22, 124–26, 127, 132; at Bath, England, 3, 8, 9, 10, 17–18; at Belfast, Ireland, 25; at Birmingham, England, 19, 28; at Boston, 134–136; at Bristol, England, 3, 9, 10, 17; at Cork, Ireland, 19; at Covent Garden, 3, 11–18, 20–25, 26–35, 39–41, 43–45; at George Town, 76, 126; at New York, 59–63, 87–90, 100–102, 110–20, 130–32; at Philadelphia, 49–58, 64–67, 71, 76–79, 83–86, 93–100, 103, 106–108, 114, 116–19, 122–24, 128–30, 133, 135; at Liverpool, England, 19; at Washington, D.C., 80–83; benefit performances, 16, 57, 58, 62 69, 72, 79, 89, 99, 102, 118; comes to the United States, 49; death of, 137–38; marries Robert Merry, 43; marries Thomas Wignell, 104; marries William Warren, 126; starring engagements, 87–90, 100–

102, 119–20, 130–32, 134–36; as manager, 108–19
—alphabetical list of plays (for more complete chronological list, *see* Appendix, pp. 147–57):
Abaellino, The Great Bandit (Rosamunda), 106, 117
Abbey of St. Augustine, The (Julia), 57
Adrian and Orilla (Madame Clermont), 136
Agreeable Surprize, The (Cowslip), 67
Alexander The Great (Statira), 26, 123, 132
Alexander The Great (Roxana), 65, 117, 120
Alfonso, King of Castile (Amelrosa), 109, 117
All For Love (Cleopatra), 34
Castle Spectre, The (Angela), 79, 123, 124
Chapter of Accidents, The (Sophia Lee), 23
Child of Nature, The (Amanthis), 29, 53, 54, 76, 78, 117
Columbus (Cora), 54, 59, 65
Conscious Lovers, The (Indiana), 26, 33
Count of Burgundy, The (Elizabeth von Hailwyl), 77
Count of Narbonne, The (Adelaide), 43
Distressed Mother, The (Hermione), 16, 17, 19, 117, 122
Dramatist, The (Louisa Courtney), 29, 31, 33, 43, 96

167